TITANIC'S LIFEBOATS

TITANIC'S LIFEBOATS

DISASTER AND SURVIVAL DURING THE LINER'S SINKING

JAMES W. BANCROFT

FRONTLINE
BOOKS

First published in Great Britain in 2025 by
Frontline Books
An imprint of
Pen & Sword Books Ltd
Yorkshire – Philadelphia

ISBN 978 1 03612 359 8

A CIP catalogue record for this book is available from the British Library.

Typeset by Lapiz Digital
Printed and bound in the UK by CPI Group (UK) Ltd, Croydon, CR0 4YY.

The Publisher's authorised representative in the EU for product safety is Authorised Rep Compliance Ltd., Ground Floor, 71 Lower Baggot Street, Dublin D02 P593, Ireland.
www.arccompliance.com

For a complete list of Pen & Sword titles please contact

PEN & SWORD BOOKS LIMITED
47 Church Street, Barnsley, South Yorkshire, S70 2AS, England
E-mail: enquiries@pen-and-sword.co.uk
Website: www.pen-and-sword.co.uk
or
PEN AND SWORD BOOKS
1950 Lawrence Road, Havertown, PA 19083, USA
E-mail: uspen-and-sword@casematepublishers.com
Website: www.penandswordbooks.com

A SELECTION OF EYEWITNESS STATEMENTS:

'How can a ship that big stay on the water?'

'That ship will always stay up in the water, Johnny!' - Frank Parkinson and his son on the day *Titanic* was launched

'Someone said we had struck an iceberg and that a huge hole had been torn in the port side below the waterline [it was actually the starboard side]. I obtained a good glimpse of the iceberg as it floated by. It was off some distance then, but in the clear night I could see it rising out of the water like a great white spectre, towering above the funnels of the ship.' – Edward Arthur Dorkings, third-class passenger

'Between one lifeboat being lowered away and the next boat being prepared, I usually nipped along to have a look down the very long emergency staircase leading direct from the boat deck down to C deck. Actually built as a short cut for the crew, it served my purpose now to gauge the speed with which the water was rising, and how high it had got. By now the foredeck was below the surface. That cold, green water crawling its ghostly way up that staircase was a sight that stamped itself indelibly on my memory. Step by step it made its way up, covering the electric lights, one after the other, which, for a time, shone under the surface with a terrible weird effect.' – Second Officer Charles Lightoller

'It was necessary for the women and children on the sinking vessel to jump 3 feet from the deck to the lifeboats. Babies were tossed into the boats. This jump had to be made 70 feet above the sea, and the height was so terrifying that some of the women refused to attempt it, and several were thrown bodily across the gap.' – Able Seaman Frank Evans

'No laughing throng, but on either side of the staircases stand quietly, bravely, the stewards all equipped with the white, ghostly life-preservers. Always the thing one tries not to see even crossing on a ferry. Now only pale faces, each form strapped about with those white bars. So gruesome a scene. We passed on. The awful goodbyes. The quiet look of hope in the brave men's eyes as the wives were put into the lifeboats. Nothing escaped one at this fearful moment. We left from the sun deck, 75 feet above the water.' – Elizabeth Weed Shutes, first-class passenger

'I shall never forget it until my dying day. There we were all huddled up together. It was awful, we could see the lights of the ship slowly disappearing beneath the waves, one by one, until there alone remained the mast light. Then suddenly the great ship gave a lurch and disappeared gracefully out of sight. All this time the people on board were shrieking in their death agonies, and the passengers were under the impression that it was the other people in the boats cheering. Only the members of the crew knew what it was and we dared not say. After the ship had gone an explosion rent the air. The shrieks of the dying were positively awful. During the time we were in the lifeboat we passed about six or seven icebergs.' – Stewardess Sarah Stap

'Before the sun rose and the dark began to slip away, I glanced around at the pale, ghostlike faces of those who survived this horrible night. But how much longer could any of us last? Was a ship coming? Then a sharp sound of a whistle grabbed our attention. Across the waves, we spotted an upside-down life-raft and rowed toward her. Standing on top of the boat were men, some looking near collapse. Carefully, they balanced themselves on the bottom of the overturned boat. The survivors were assisted into our lifeboats, and still holding onto hope, I searched for my father's face. When I saw that Dad was not among them, I cried. Then blue lights appeared in the sky – rockets. A ship came into view. At last, we were saved!' – Alice Phillips, second-class passenger

'It wasn't long before they let down a little wooden seat [from CS *Carpathia*] about 2 feet long and a foot wide. Men on the deck held the ends of the cables to which this seat was attached. The lifeboat was bobbing up and down on the waves and it was pretty hard to stand up in it long enough to climb out to the seat, but you can wager we all did it. After we picked up all the lifeboats we steamed again about the scene of the disaster. In among the glassy, towering peaks of ice we threaded our way, seeing a bit of wreckage here and a baby's bonnet or a man's glove there, but no boats, and at noon we turned toward Ambrose lightship and home.' – Caroline Bonnell, first-class passenger

'The sea was dotted with bodies as far as one could see, and the decks were covered with them. Everybody had on a lifebelt and bodies floated very high in the water in spite of the sodden clothes and things in pockets. Apparently, the people had lots of time and discipline must have been splendid, for some had on their pyjamas, two and three shirts, two pairs of pants, two vests, two jackets and an overcoat. In some pockets a quantity of meat and biscuits were found, while in the pockets of most of the crew quite a lot of tobacco and matches besides keys to the various lockers and stateroom doors were found. On this day we buried fifteen bodies some of them very badly smashed and bruised.' – A *Carpathia* spokesman

'Terrible, terrible. No pen can ever depict and no tongue can ever describe adequately the terrors of our experience. Everywhere was a cold, hopeless despair and grief in its most hellish form. Some were dumb with horror; others beat their breasts like things crazed, and a few laughed hysterically and insanely.' – William Ernest Carter, first-class passenger

'It is not because it was the largest and most luxurious ship in the world. Quite simply, it is because the *Titanic* is the one and only disaster – land, sea and air – for which there was no excuse for anyone to die. It was the murder of 1,516 people who had to die because there were not any lifeboats... a dreadful waste of life.' – Eva Hart, second-class passenger

CONTENTS

INTRODUCTION

I have produced this work with the intention of being informative, particularly concerning the general reader. I have tried to interpret the events as I see them in my mind's eye, and to steer away from any attempt to analyse any aspect of the RMS *Titanic* disaster. I have studied the various eyewitness accounts for five decades, many of them being understandably contradictory considering the peril the passengers and crew were in, and the narrative is my interpretation of what I believe happened during the dreadful events as each lifeboat was launched from the doomed ship. In most cases I have avoided any effort to scrutinise what time each event took place or the number of individuals in each lifeboat. Most importantly, I have tried to do the victims and survivors a service of respect in turning them into identifiable and relatable human beings who became involved in what must surely be one of the saddest incidents in history, and from which most of the people who survived the disaster never really recovered.

People from all walks of life who boarded the luxury liner RMS *Titanic* at Southampton on the south coast of England, or Cherbourg in northern France, on 10 April 1912, and Queenstown (now Cobh) in southern Ireland, on the following day, felt privileged to be part of her maiden voyage, but what they did not know was that it was destined to be the only voyage.

While pushing relentlessly westward through the waves at full steam ahead across the North Atlantic Ocean towards New York on the night of 14/15 April 1912, the ship collided with a frozen mass of ice. Evidence suggests that she struck the iceberg three times in quick succession, causing a series of large gashes or punctures which were dotted along about 300 feet of the starboard front side; about a third of her total length. She sank in less than three hours, taking about two out of every three of her passengers and crew with her – a terrible loss of life.

Disturbed from safety, peace and comfort, many passengers who enquired about the situation after the collision were reassured by members of the crew that nothing serious had happened and were told to go back to their cabins, and even to go back to bed. However, it is difficult to comprehend how they must have felt when they realised the peril they were in as distress flares went up and the lifeboats were uncovered and prepared for launch. What effect did it have on them to hear the piteous cries of children, some of whom were forced from family members, and the screams of heartbroken wives as they were taken from the arms of their husbands, leaving them to a certain and awful death. It was a less certain destiny for the people who managed to get into the lifeboats. Where were they supposed to go? Were they expected to row all the way to New York?

The White Star Line never envisaged that the passengers and crew would have to be evacuated all at once, and the lifeboats were intended to be used to transfer passengers off the stricken ship to a nearby vessel that had hopefully arrived to offer assistance. The view of the time was that 'every ship should be her own lifeboat' and the Olympic class ships were constructed with sixteen watertight compartments that could be isolated from each other from controls at the Bridge. When the collision occurred, six of them were exposed to the sea, and although they could prevent the water from rushing to the rest of the ship, the assessment put forward by Professor John Harvard Biles of the Institute of Naval Architecture soon after the sinking, suggests that the weight of the water was not taken into consideration. The amount of water that filled the compartments was enough to cause the ship to list quite dramatically, thus allowing gallons of water to rush onto the decks one by one as they sank beneath the surface, pulling the ship down in stages as it did so. The pressure of this forced the hull plates to split open and continue cracking as the water flooded in.

Officers took time to assess the damage, although evidence suggests they realised the ship was doomed when the wheelhouse instruments indicated a 5-degree list not long after the collision, and there was nothing they could do about it. When they eventually decided to evacuate, they were working against the clock, and more valuable time was lost when many passengers were reluctant to leave their loved ones behind and get off the massive 'unsinkable' ship into the comparatively small lifeboats, the first of which was not launched until about an hour after the collision. The general sequence they followed when launching the lifeboats was front starboard first, then front portside, followed by rear starboard, and rear portside, and then the collapsible rafts towards the front of the ship.

By the time all the lifeboats at the front of the ship had been launched, *Titanic* was already low in the water in that area, and as each launch had to be supervised by an officer, of which there were only seven, not including the captain, it is likely that even if there had been more lifeboats there would not have been enough time to get them all away. Indeed, if the weather had caused a rough sea, experts believed it would have been impossible to launch any of the lifeboats and there would probably have been no survivors.

At the British inquiry, Sir Alfred Chambers of the Board of Trade was of the opinion that '...if there had been fewer lifeboats on *Titanic* then more people would have been saved. If there had been fewer lifeboats then more people would have rushed to the boats and they would have been filled to capacity and thus saving more lives.' However, this is not necessarily a correct assumption.

As many people in the lifeboats watched with dread as they rowed away, the listing of the ship became severe, and then it began to lurch forward now and again as the front sank deeper and deeper into the icy water. There were several loud explosions, which blew many people overboard and into a watery grave, and the fourth funnel, which served only as a ventilation shaft, became loose and crashed down into the sea, crushing many more people – perhaps mercifully. Finally, the ship split in two and seemed to slide downwards as it disappeared beneath the surface.

Eyewitnesses remembered that whenever lifeboats came near to each other, passengers would shout names across from one to the other hoping for a reply – but there was none. There was nothing to eat or drink in most of the lifeboats, and they could do nothing more than wait in the freezing-cold air and hope that a rescue ship was on its way – and pray that it could find them.

The CS *Carpathia* was travelling from New York to Gibraltar and fortunately was in the region, and on receiving a distress signal from *Titanic* it immediately set a course towards the disaster area. After working through dangerous ice fields, it arrived at the scene at 4am on 15 April and saved over 700 people.

Soon after *Carpathia* had landed back in New York, a committee of the surviving passengers put out the following statement:

> At 11:40 on the evening of Sunday, April 14, on a cold and starlit night, the *Titanic* struck an iceberg. The look-outs reported the iceberg before the collision, but the vessel was unable to avoid it. Orders were promptly given to put on lifebelts, and the lifeboats were launched and distress signals sent out by wireless and rockets fired.
>
> The vessel sank at 2:20 am, on Monday. The *Carpathia* arrived at 4 am and took the rescued passengers from the boats. The captain and

> officers of the *Carpathia* gave the most touching care and attention to all the passengers when they were taken on board.
>
> Every individual on board had been allocated a life-jacket, but the ship carried fourteen lifeboats, two smaller boats, and four collapsible boats. The boats were entirely insufficient to enable all those on board to escape.
>
> There was no panic on board while the women and children were leaving the ship in the boats; everyone believed that it was simply a measure of precaution. Several women were torn from their husbands when the orders were given to rescue only the women. Even then several refused to leave and were drowned with their husbands. One woman died in a lifeboat, and three others succumbed after reaching the *Carpathia*.

The first lifeboat to reach *Carpathia* was emergency lifeboat 2 at just after 4am on 15 April 1912, and Emilie Kreuchen, a German-born personal maid, was the first to climb on board. Emergency lifeboat 1 arrived at the rescue ship not long afterwards.

The largest contingent of victims came from or lived in Southampton. It was the hometown of most of the crew, and as many as 500 households in the town lost at least one family member or lodger. Liverpool was also badly affected by the enormous loss of life of people from that city, and the disaster cast a shadow over many areas of Britain in some way or another.

When asked by newspapers for his opinion concerning the RMS *Titanic* disaster, Captain Roald Amundsen, who had just conquered the South Pole, stated:

> 'It is improbable that the iceberg was a mile long,' and thinks, 'that there was probably a long line of icebergs'. He accounted for the presence of icebergs in the locality as early as being due to abnormally strong wind in the north several weeks previously. He was reticent when questioned as to the possibility of ascertaining the proximity of icebergs. He however said that one measure was to take the temperature regularly. 'One thing was certain,' said Captain Amundsen, 'at the conclusion of the inquiry; it would be found that Captain Smith and his officers had done their duty.'

Regulations governing the number of lifeboats required on passenger ships had not been revised since 1896. The lifeboats were designed by Scottish draughtsman Roderick Chisholm (1868–1912) and constructed at the Harland and Wolff shipyard in Belfast, where RMS *Titanic* itself was built. The ship was designed to carry thirty-two lifeboats, but the number was reduced to twenty because it was considered that the top deck would be too cluttered. There were three types of lifeboats on board. The fourteen regular wooden boats were approximately 30 feet long, 9 feet wide, and 4 feet deep. Two wooden cutters were used as emergency vessels, already hanging in their crane-like devices (davits) for incidents such as someone falling overboard and struggling in the sea. They were smaller, at about 25 feet long, 7 feet wide, and 3 feet deep. Four shallow clinker-built boats with collapsible canvas sides were about 28 feet long, 8 feet wide, and 14 inches deep; and had to be launched by using the same davits as the regular lifeboats after they had been launched.

The various types of lifeboats were all stored in six separate areas of the top deck. Looking towards the front of the ship, numbers 7, 5, 3 and emergency 1 were at the front, starboard (right) hand side, with numbers 4, 6, 8 and emergency 2 at the front, portside (left) hand side. Numbers 9, 11, 13 and 15 were at the rear starboard side, and numbers 10, 12, 14 and 16 at the rear portside. Rafts C and D could be accessed much easier than the other two because they were stored in their collapsed state underneath the cutters close to the emergency lifeboats on each side of the front of the ship. However, the collapsible rafts lettered A and B were stored on each side of the top of the officers' quarters behind the wheelhouse at the front of the ship. They were about 8 feet above the deck and lowering them required a piece of equipment which was held in the botswain's store at the front of the ship. By the time it came for these two lifeboats to be accessed, the bow was already under water, and as they were released, they were washed off the deck.

It was considered that the fourteen wooden lifeboats were capable of carrying sixty-five people in each, for a total of 896; with forty each in the two emergency lifeboats, for a total of eighty, and forty-seven in each of the four collapsible dinghies, for a total of 188; making a grand total of 1,164 people; already dreadfully insufficient for the number of passengers on board. However, some experts later suggested that if stricter safety regulations had been in force at the time of the vessel's construction, none of the twenty lifeboats were capable of carrying more than forty people in safety, which was a maximum of 800. It is difficult to comprehend, but at the time of the disaster lifeboat accommodation was regulated according to the tonnage of the ship and not the number of persons on board. With these figures in mind, it would seem that in practice, the lifeboats were not seaworthy if they had more than forty passengers in them. Adding to the problem was the fact that the crew had not been sufficiently trained in the use of the davits – the lifeboat launching equipment.

Alfred Omont was in lifeboat 7, the first to be lowered, and he stated his concerns: 'The boat could not have held more than thirty in any case. I personally consider and state that the idea of putting sixty people in a boat or on a raft is ridiculous. I have a photograph in my possession which shows how ridiculous it is to attempt to put fifty or sixty persons in one of these boats or rafts. I consider it a monstrosity to state that one could put sixty persons in a boat safely.'

Several London newspapers for 17 June 1912 reported: '*Titanic's* Lifeboats – A Neglected Recommendation':

> In giving evidence today before the special committee of inquiry into the loss of the *Titanic,* Mr Archer, principal ship surveyor to the Board of Trade, said that if recommendations made by him in 1911 had been adopted, they would have given the *Titanic* lifeboat accommodation for nearly 3,000 persons. The rule exempting vessels with watertight bulkheads from the boat regulation ought to be abandoned. Boat accommodation should be regulated according to the number of persons on board, instead of the tonnage. A committee should be appointed to consider the methods of lowering boats.

Under the title 'The *Titanic's* Lifeboats' the *Adelaide Register* for 18 April 1912 carried this quite alarming statement:

> Mr Alexander McCowan (Lloyd's surveyor, of Melbourne), speaking from memory, states that for mail liners such as those employed in the Australian trade, the Board of Trade rules stipulate for lifesaving equipment equal probably to about half the vessel's complement of passengers and crew. In regard to such a colossal and well-found liner as the *Titanic,* the Board of Trade's demands would not be more than this. All the boats having been filled with passengers until no more could be taken; it would appear that the others had to be left to take their chances on the ship.

An equally disturbing report appeared in the *Sydney Sun* for 7 June 1912, under the title: 'Ocean Liner's Lifeboats – The *Titanic's* Equipment – White Star Director's Views:

> Harold Sanderson, one of the directors of the White Star Line, stated today that if, as a result of the *Titanic* inquiry, the shipping companies were ordered to man their vessels with able-bodied sailors, it would simply mean asking them to get for their ships a type of seamen that did not exist in the country.
>
> He expressed the opinion that it would be impracticable for a ship like the *Titanic* to accommodate the full number of lifeboats required for

a vessel of her magnitude. Mr Sanderson went on to say that even in fine weather, the lifeboats were not sea worthy when loaded with 65 persons. The most the boats would carry was 40, and in rough weather it was impossible to even launch them.

Under the heading 'Safety of Life' – 'Lifeboats at Sea' – 'Lessons of the *Titanic*', the *Sydney Morning Herald* for 29 May 1929, reported:

The subject of boats and other life-saving appliances on passenger ships has been under consideration by a committee of the International Conference on Safety of Life at Sea, now sitting in London. At the previous International Conference, held in 1914, which followed the loss of the *Titanic*, very great public interest was taken on this question. The lifeboats on the *Titanic* were sufficient for 1,178 persons, but only 652 left the *Titanic* in boats out of a total of 2,201 persons on board. Popular demand was for boats for all, and the conference made provision to meet this demand. For some years past practically all ocean-going passenger ships have been required to comply with the convention standard as regards the number of lifeboats carried. Experience gained since 1914, however, has shown the prime necessity for boats being carried so as to be readily available for launching. It has also proved that where this requirement is not complied with, the provision of a large number of lifeboats may be a source of danger. The life-saving appliances committee has, therefore, kept before it two main principles - firstly, that all life-saving appliances on a ship shall be readily available: and, secondly, that they shall be adequate.

On these matters the committee's proposals are, firstly, that every lifeboat on board should be so carried as to be readily available in emergency: and no boat should be carried which will impede the prompt handling of the boats that are available: and, secondly, that these readily available boats on ocean-going passenger ships should provide accommodation for all persons on board.

In addition, the committee proposes that light, buoyant apparatus be provided which will float in the sea and provide persons with something to which they can cling if, by reason of the rapid sinking of a vessel, it has been impossible to get them away on the boats. Such apparatus is a definite additional measure of safety, and is to be provided in determined proportion to the number of persons on board. Regarding the use of life rafts, it has been found that on certain special voyages life rafts have proved to be of greater service than inboard boats. The committee contemplates that administrations might, if satisfied that rafts will be more useful than boats, allow rafts in substitution for boats over and above a certain specified minimum accommodation in the lifeboats, such minimum being sufficient to ensure that in the North Atlantic passenger trade, and in most of the other trades, lifeboat accommodation shall be

> provided for all. In view of the improved reliability of motor lifeboats, the committee expresses the opinion that, where more than a certain number of lifeboats are carried, one or more should be motor boats fitted with wireless installations and searchlights.

The *Titanic* disaster is one of history's most catastrophic human tragedies, which harbours many heartbreaking stories about its ill-fated passengers and crew, whose lives were painfully shattered by what they saw and experienced during that one dreadful incident. The *New York Times* was of the opinion that, 'The tremendous and overwhelming disaster to the *Titanic* was the greatest blow that has come to America since the beginning of the Civil War fifty years ago.'

What happened to the ship and its victims is now planted firmly within the national consciousness. The disaster caused widespread outrage because of the lack of lifeboats, and subsequent enquiries recommended sweeping changes to maritime regulations, leading to the establishment of the International Convention for the Safety of Life at Sea (SOLAS).

James W. Bancroft, 2025

A PERFECT PARTNERSHIP

Edward Harland (1831–1895) was employed as the general manager for the company of Robert Hickson (1815–1869) at his shipyard at Queen's Island in Belfast, and after buying the concern in 1858 he named it Edward James Harland and Company. In 1860 he formed a business partnership with his former personal assistant Gustav Wolff (1834–1913), whose uncle was an investor at John Bibby (1775–1840) & Sons of Liverpool. The first three ships in the newly incorporated shipyard of Harland & Wolff were for that line and were named *Venetian, Sicilian* and *Syrian*. Bibby's were impressed with the boats, and soon ordered another six.

Edward Harland's father was a physician and an amateur engineer. He patented a multi-tube steam-powered carriage and constructed a set of dentures for himself by grinding down the teeth of a hippopotamus. Coming from such an inventive father it was not surprising that Edward made a success of the ship-building business through several innovations. He replaced wooden upper-decks with ones made of iron, which increased the sturdiness of the ships, and gave the hulls squarer bottoms, which increased their capacity. The Harland & Wolff-constructed ships came to be known as 'Bibby's Coffins'.

At the turn of the century, the Harland & Wolff shipyard was described by the Irish journalist Bram Stoker (1847–1912), of 'Dracula' fame, as the greatest shipyard in the world; and as confirmation of the durability of the Queen's Island ships, under the heading 'Harland and Wolff's First Steamer', the *Daily Commercial News and Shipping List* in Sydney for 21 November 1910, reported, 'What is said to be the first steamer turned out by the well-known ship building firm of Harland and Wolff, of Belfast – the trawler *Mollogh,* 55 years ago – is at present undergoing her annual overhaul at Lyttelton [New Zealand]. Her engines are still in good condition, although of obsolete design.'

***

The White Star Line was established in 1845. It began the business of shipbrokers in Liverpool, from where it initially leased and chartered ships to operate packet sailing to the east coast of the United States. It started to use the name White Star Line of Boston Packets in 1849 but cut it short to just White Star Line after it started sending ships to Australia. Business increased after the discovery of gold in Australia in 1851, and this enabled the company to purchase the vessels it used.

However, the company's bank failed in 1867 and with massive debts it was forced into bankruptcy. However, in the following year Thomas Henry Ismay (1837–1899) purchased the bankrupt company, with the intention of operating large steamships on the North Atlantic service between Liverpool and New York.

During a game of billiards, Ismay was approached by Gustav Wolff and his uncle, who offered to finance the new line. A partnership with Harland & Wolff was established in the summer of 1869, the agreement being that Harland & Wolff would build ships exclusively for the White Star Line. On the death of Thomas in 1899, he was succeeded as the chairman and managing director of the White Star Line by his son, Joseph Bruce Ismay (1862–1937), known as Bruce. In 1907 Bruce met Lord William Pirrie (1847–1924) of Harland & Wolff, to discuss White Star Line's answer to Cunard Line's recently unveiled *Lusitania* and *Mauretania.* They came up with the idea of building three 'Olympic Class' ships at Harland & Wolff that were intended to be marvels of engineering.

When information concerning the new ships became public, and that they would be built at Harland & Wolff in Belfast, local Press lauded: 'There is great satisfaction in Belfast of the prospect of assured work for a considerable period being given by the building of two mammoth White Star liners. It is estimated that at least £2,000,000 will be spent in wages in Belfast. Twelve thousand men are employed in Messrs Harland and Wolfe's [*sic*] shipyards, the wages bill reaching £18,000 a week.'

The three ships planned for the Olympic Class would focus on comfort and luxury over speed, with lavishly decorated rooms, and passenger facilities were to be of the highest standard. They would be fitted with special gears which would reduce vibration from being transmitted to the rest of the ship and the passengers. Simply by pulling a lever on the Bridge it was possible to close sixteen compartments within the vessel so that if water was to enter in some way, it would be contained within these compartments.

The ship was designed to provide the ultimate in luxury travel. The first-class smoking room was one of the grandest areas on the ship.

It was decorated with intricately carved dark mahogany wood, which was inlaid with mother-of-pearl patterns, red and blue linoleum tiles, and stained-glass windows. The interior windows were illuminated by electric lights. There was a swimming pool with an adjacent Turkish bath suite, a state-of-the-art gymnasium, an à la carte restaurant, and the Café Parisien. However, the ship's main feature was the grand staircase. Built from solid English oak and enhanced with wrought iron, the decorated glass domes above were designed to let in as much natural light as possible. To have sailed on 'The voyage of the century' aboard RMS *Titanic,* the world's largest and most luxurious vessel afloat at that time, was like being one of the first people to fly on Concorde. It was described at the time as 'a floating palace' – a combination of Mayfair and Bel Air on water!

The first of these 'unsinkable' ships was named RMS *Olympic.* It was ordered in 1907 and construction began on 16 December 1908. The ship was launched on 20 October 1910, completed on 31 May 1911 (the same day RMS *Titanic* was launched), and began her maiden voyage to New York on 14 June 1911, reaching her destination a week later.

During her fifth voyage on 20 September 1911, *Olympic,* with Captain Edward Smith and Officer William Murdoch on board, had a serious collision with the British cruiser HMS *Hawke.* A subsequent inquiry found that *Olympic* was at fault for the collision.

The second ship in the class, to be named RMS *Titanic,* was ordered on 17 September 1908 and laid down for construction on 31 March 1909. The ship was launched on 31 May 1911.

On 3 February 1912, *Titanic* was dry docked, the move taking a little more than two hours. She would remain in the dock for two weeks, while furnishing of her interiors continued. The primary reason for dry docking was to fit her three giant propellers and a final preparation of the hull for the sea; this involved cleaning the hull below the waterline and applying red antifouling paint.

However, on 6 March 1912 *Titanic* was moved out of dry dock to allow for *Olympic* to have a propeller blade fixed, which had become damaged during the collision with HMS *Hawke.* Consequently, *Titanic* was not completed until 2 April 1912 and was fatefully re-scheduled to begin her maiden voyage on Wednesday, 10 April 1912.

SEAWORTHY?

The sea trials for *Titanic* were arranged to take place on 1 April but were postponed because of high winds and were conducted on 2 April instead. Second Officer Charles Lightoller (1874–1952) said they took place in Belfast Lough, where the weather was clear and good, but for a light breeze; but Third Officer Herbert Pitman (1877–1961) testified that some of the trials took place in the open sea [Irish Sea].

The trials consisted of turning the ship in circles to see what space it would turn under certain helms, with the engines at various speeds, and while adjusting the compass. This took about five hours. Then the vessel was driven full speed ahead for two hours out along the 15-mile-long lough, and two more hours back; the fastest speed attained was apparently 23 knots. The final test was full speed astern, to see at what distance the ship would stop with the engines at full speed when going backwards.

At that time First Officer William Murdoch (1873–1912) instructed his fellow officers to check the lifeboats and their equipment. During the United States Senate inquiry, Officer Lowe stated:

> Sixth Officer James Moody [1887–1912] and myself and Third Officer Pitman and Fourth Officer Joseph Boxhall [1884–1967] took the port boat – that is, I took the starboard, and they took the port, and we overhauled them; that is to say, we counted the oars, the rowlocks, or the hole pins, whichever you like to call them, and saw there was a mast and sail, rigging, gear, and everything else that fitted in the boat, and plugs, and also that the biscuit tank was all right, and that there were two breakers in the boat, two bailers, two plugs, and the steering rowlock, that is, the rowlock for the oar that you ship aft where there is a heavy sea running, because you can't steer by rudder when there is a heavy sea running, and you put an oar over and you have greater command over an oar and can put more power on it.
>
> Everything was absolutely correct with the exception of one dipper. A dipper is a long thin can about that length [indicating] and about that diameter [indicating] – an inch and a quarter diameter – and you

> drop it down into the water breaker and draw the water. That was the only thing that was short out of our boats, and our boats were respectively, numbers 1, 3, 5, 7, 9, 11, 13, and 15, from 1 to 15 – odd numbers. Then the even numbers were on the other side, that is, on the portside of the ship.
>
> We found 14 oars, and anyhow, a set and a half of oars on one set of rowlocks. That is, if there were six rowlocks, there were nine oars in case of emergency. That is, if an oar got broke there was another extra oar to replace that oar, and there were three spare ones – that is, one and a half sets. If there were 12 oars in one boat, it was fully equipped. There would be 18 oars altogether – six extras – and dippers and everything else. Everything was absolutely correct; I will swear to that. There is a compass, a light, and oil to burn for eight hours; biscuits and water. That is all I can think of at present.

The first man to command RMS *Titanic* was Captain Herbert Haddock (1861–1946), as the ship set off on its delivery voyage from Belfast and arrived at Southampton during the first hour of 4 April 1912. At Southampton, Captain Edward Smith (1850–1912) took over command of the ship. By midday men were turning up at the dock to sign on as members of the crew, many of them having transferred to *Titanic* for her maiden voyage because the coal strike had delayed other ships. She made a majestic sight as she was moored for five days in Berth 43 at Dock Gate 4, the entrance to the Eastern Dock in Southampton.

In his 1936 book *Titanic and Other Ships*, Charles Lightoller recorded:

> Unfortunately, whilst in Southampton we had a re-shuffle amongst the senior officers, owing to the *Olympic* being laid up, the ruling lights of the White Star Line thought it would be a good plan to send the chief officer of the *Olympic*, just for one voyage, as chief officer of the *Titanic*, to help, with his experience of her sister ship. This doubtful policy threw both Murdoch and me out of our stride; and apart from the disappointment of having to step back in our rank, caused quite a little confusion. Murdoch from chief, took over my duties as First, I stepped back on Officer David Blair's toes, as Second, and picked up the many threads of his job, whilst he – luckily for him as it turned out – was left behind. The other officers remained the same. However, a couple of days in Southampton saw each of us settled in our new positions and familiar with our duties.

Officer Blair left the ship on 9 April, and as it was due to sail on the following day he would have been rushing about getting ready to disembark. In his rush he forgot to hand over the key to the locker which contained the binoculars for the lookouts in the crow's nest. It was to be hoped they did not get into any difficulty which would require them. His daughter wrote: 'In the rush to pack his belongings and get off before she sailed, he came away with a key in his pocket and there was no opportunity to return it.'

Lawrence Beesley, a Derbyshire-born science teacher at Dulwich College, and second-class passenger who survived the disaster in lifeboat 13, stated:

> I went on board at Southampton at 10am, Wednesday, April 10, after staying the night in the town. It is pathetic to recall that as I sat that morning in the breakfast room of an hotel, from the windows of which could be seen the four huge funnels of the *Titanic* towering over the roofs of the various shipping offices opposite, and the procession of stokers and stewards wending their way to the ship. There sat behind me three of the *Titanic's* passengers discussing the coming voyage, and estimating, among other things, the probabilities of an accident at sea to the ship.
>
> Just before the last gangway was withdrawn a knot of stokers ran along the quay, with their kit slung over their shoulders and bundles, and made for the gangway, with the evident intention of joining the ship. But a petty officer guarding the shore end of the gangway firmly refused to allow them on board; they argued, gesticulated, apparently attempting to explain the reasons why they were late, but he remained obdurate and waved them back with a determined hand, and the gangway was dragged back amid their protests...

Miss Roberta Maioni, maid to the Countess of Rothes, remembered, 'We passengers were crushed and pushed about by excited crowds as we struggled to reach the gangway, but once across we were swallowed up in that great vessel. The noise made in getting the luggage aboard was deafening, but when the *Titanic* started on its journey an even greater pandemonium broke loose – the cheering of thousands of people and the shrieking of many sirens.'

There was a variety of items stored in the ship's cargo hold. These included a 1912 Renault Type CB Coupe de Ville, and some polo ponies, which belonged to William Ernest Carter.

It is my belief that the cursed lid of the sarcophagus which is said to have once contained the remains of Tcheser-Ka-Ra, the High Priestess Amen-Ra of Thebes was on *Titanic*. It had been the cause of many strange happenings and unfortunate accidents for centuries, including a number of mishaps causing injury to the employees of the British Museum, where it was on display in the Egyptian Room.

Because of these accidents, and unknown to the public, the cover was removed to the cellars of the museum and replaced by a replica. However, a visiting American Egyptologist inspected the lid and his expert eye discovered that it was not the original. Fearing criticism that the museum was displaying a fake artefact, they showed him the original and after suggesting that such an exhibit should not be wasted hidden away in a basement, the man bought the coffin lid 'For America'. It was packed away and taken on board RMS *Titanic.*

The commercial cargo manifest for *Titanic* does not record the presence of an Egyptian coffin lid, but as newspaper reports explain, 'It was packed carefully, so that no one could guess what its covering-case contained; and arrangements were made that no hitch would he caused by Customs House examinations.' The manifest included several cases easily large enough to contain the coffin lid, and it could have been secreted in one of the general commercial cases, such as that of the American Express Company, which included '25 cases of merchandise' – the contents of which were not specified. And so the coffin lid was despatched to America, but did the lid's reputed diabolic power cause the ship to founder?

Dr William O'Loughlin, a 62-year-old Irishman, was senior surgeon with the White Star Line. Just before the ship had set sail on 10 April, he, along with Dr Edward Simpson and Captain Maurice Clarke, the Board of Trade immigration officer, had examined the crew muster sheets to ensure a healthy crew was aboard. They, of course, were not to know that two of the crew had spent time in prison for taking the life of another.

Able Seaman Joe Scarrott stated, 'On joining a ship all sailors have much the same routine. You go to your quarters, choose your bunk, and get the gear you require from your bag. Then you change into your uniform. By that time you are called to muster by the chief officer.'

The cabin or bedroom stewards and stewardesses are employed with keeping rooms tidy and ready for passengers, and all other types of room service, including carrying luggage to rooms when a guest first arrives. In addition to cleaning the rooms, keeping beds tidy, replacing towels, and other basic services, the cabin steward also provides information to guests and help to improve their experiences on the ship. All employees on a ship should be trustworthy, but as a cabin steward is often in a passenger's room, these employees must be particularly friendly, honest, professional, and polite. They are usually responsible for the upkeep of a set of rooms, most often in the same general area. The stewardesses on *Titanic* worked as many as seventeen hours per shift, and with wages of £3 10s a month they were among the lowest paid on the ship.

Men would receive £6 a month for working as firemen/stokers in the engine room, where their duties included feeding the furnaces with coal brought to them by trimmers. There were twenty-nine boilers, which powered the three massive engines. The men who worked in this department were known as the 'Black Gang' because of their dirty appearance, and they were rarely seen by the passengers.

Titanic's bunkers were set up so that trimmers did not need to wheel the coal to the firemen as they did in some other ships. There was a bunker door opposite each boiler, so that the firemen could just turn around and scoop up the coal. Trimmers were still needed to haul away the ash from the boilers. About once a watch the ash would be pulled out of each furnace and dumped on the plates in front of the boiler. The trimmer had to cool the ash with a hose and cart it to the ash ejectors, where it was fired into the sea by a high-pressure jet of water. Trimmers were also needed to remove coal from remote parts of the bunkers and keep the supply near the bunkers full.

There were four trimmers in each boiler room, one fireman for each of the ten boiler ends, and a leading fireman in overall charge of the boiler room. All the boiler rooms were supervised by a senior engineer. Each fireman had three furnaces to tend, and it was hard but skilled work. It was a lot more than just shovelling coal, and a good, experienced fireman could use half the coal of an unskilled man, while many had learned to keep the doors closed because of the intense heat.

Even the seventeen greasers who lubricated the engines on *Titanic* had a daunting task. Imagine a block of metal the size of a car engine revolving so quickly that you cannot even follow it with your eye; then imagine trying to stroke it as it flirts by with a rag full of grease.

The only drill that took place while the vessel was docked at Southampton, or indeed during the voyage, consisted of filling lifeboats 11 and 13 with a few men on the starboard side and dropping them down the side of the ship and into the water, and these boats were again hoisted to the boat deck within half an hour. No boat list was posted which clearly designated where members of the crew should be stationed in the event of an emergency until several days after sailing from Southampton, and few knew their proper stations until the following Friday morning.

Fireman / Stoker John Dilley, an ex-army man stated:

> From the day we sailed the *Titanic* was on fire, in bunker 6, and my sole duty, together with eleven other men, had been to fight that fire. We had made no headway against it. Of course the passengers knew nothing of the fire. There were hundreds of tons of coal stored there. The coal on top of the bunker was wet, as all of the coal should have been, but down at the bottom of the bunker the coal was dry. The coal at the bottom of the bunker took fire and smouldered for days. The wet coal on the top kept the flames from coming through, but down in the bottom of the bunker the flames were raging. Two men from each watch of stokers were told off to fight the fire. The stokers worked four hours at a time, so 12 of us were fighting the flames from the day we put out of Southampton till we hit the iceberg.

As a member of the Guarantee Group, who went on ship maiden voyages to observe what improvements could be made about the ship and its facilities, Thomas Andrews, a Belfast man who was a managing director of Harland & Wolff, spent most of his voyage on *Titanic* making notes. He usually dined on the next table to a twice-married New Yorker named Eleanor Cassebeer, and she later stated he had mentioned to her that: 'the vessel was started on her maiden voyage before she was finished.' However, he also stated that the ship was: 'as nearly perfect as human brains can make her.'

THE FATEFUL VOYAGE

RMS *Titanic's* departure on 10 April 1912 was almost marred by a disaster. Leaving her dock soon after noon, *Titanic* was pulled out into Southampton Water by three tugs. As the vast ship moved along the quay, she passed the liner *Oceanic,* with a distance of about 50 yards separating the vessels, then she came opposite the liner *New York.* The seven ropes holding the *New York* to the quay began to strain, and she was being drawn towards *Titanic* by suction. Suddenly, some of the ropes snapped and the stern of the vessel began to veer round towards *Titanic.* The great ship came to a standstill, and as soon as the rope had been disconnected, the three tugs went to the assistance of the *New York.* At this time barely 15 feet separated the two vessels. Fortunately, the tugs were able to secure the *New York* and get her back to the quay. *Titanic* backed up about 200 yards, and eventually the three tugs were connected to her again. Another start was made, and this time the other ships were passed without mishap.

Albert Ervine was an electrician, the youngest man in the engineering department, who was working on the top of the back funnel of *Titanic* with his older friend and fellow electrician Alfred Middleton, and they both had a good panoramic view of the collision. He wrote a letter to his mother while he was on his way from Cherbourg to Queenstown and posted it when he arrived. It showed that he had complete confidence in the ship, but it contained a somewhat poignant last line. It stated:

> Yours received at Cherbourg, France, yesterday evening. We have had everything working nicely so far, except when leaving Southampton. As soon as the *Titanic* began to move out of the dock, the suction caused the *Oceanic,* which was alongside her birth, to swing outwards, while another liner *(New York)* broke loose altogether and bumped into the *Oceanic.* The gangway of the *Oceanic* simply dissolved. Middleton and myself were on the top of the aft funnel, so we saw everything quite distinctly. I thought there was going to be a proper smash up owing to the high wind; but I don't think anyone was hurt.

> Well, we were at Cherbourg last night. It was just a mass of fortifications. We are on our way to County Cork. The next call then is New York. I am on duty morning and evening from 8 to 12; that is four hours work and eight hours off (have just been away attending the alarm bell). This morning we had a full dress rehearsal of an emergency. The alarm bells all rang for ten seconds, then about fifty doors, all steel, gradually slid down into their places, so that water could not escape from one section to the next.
>
> So you see it would be impossible for the ship to be sunk in collision with another.

First-class passenger Adolphe Saalfeld related: 'After leaving at noon we had quite a little excitement, as the tremendous suction of the steamer made all the hawsers of the SS *New York* snap as we passed her and she drifted on to our boat, a collision being averted by our stopping, and our tugs coming to the rescue of the *New York*.'

Lawrence Beesley noted, 'In our wake soared and screamed hundreds of gulls', and Roberta Maioni recalled how a large flock of seagulls followed the ship out to sea, which someone pointed out to her was a sign of impending disaster. Her family state that 20-year-old Roberta and a young steward became fond of each other during the voyage, but his identity is not known. He gave her a star-shaped enamel brooch, which still exists, which he is said to have bought from a barber shop on the ship.

A civil engineer named Edward Colley, a veteran of the Klondike gold rush in Canada, who was on his way to Vancouver to work as a consultant to a prominent British Columbia industrialist, stated, 'This is a huge ship. Unless lots of people get on at Cherbourg and Queenstown they'll never half fill it.'

Mr Saalfeld continued:

> At 6pm we anchored outside Cherbourg and two tugs with passengers came alongside. Owing to our little mishap at Southampton we were all an hour late and had dinner only at 7:30pm instead of seven o'clock as usual. After a fair night's rest and an excellent breakfast I am enjoying a promenade in glorious weather. The wind is fresh and the sea moderate, but on this big boat one hardly notices any movement. I write these lines just before we are getting into Queenstown so that you get them tomorrow morning. I shall not be able to write to you again before getting to New York.

The harbour at Cherbourg-Octeville was the second largest artificial harbour in the world at that time, and *Titanic* sailed into it in the early evening of 10 April. An hour and a half later two tenders named *Nomadic* and *Traffic* had brought 281 passengers to the ship to be embarked, and when the task was completed, *Titanic* set sail for Queenstown. While waiting for the tender to pick them up at Cherbourg, Emma Bucknell, a wealthy Philadelphia widow, who was travelling with her Italian maid Albina Bassani, told an old acquaintance of hers named Margaret 'Molly' Brown, that she had 'evil forebodings' that something might happen to the ship. Mrs Brown laughed it off.

Thomas Andrews was popular with the crew, and during the voyage Chief Baker Charles Joughin had prepared for him a special loaf of bread. He wrote a note from Cherbourg to his wife: 'We reached here in nice time and took on board quite a number of passengers. The two little tenders looked well; you will remember we built them about a year ago. We expect to arrive at Queenstown about 10:30am tomorrow. The weather is fine and everything shaping for a good voyage. I have a seat at the doctor's table.'

Tommie Andrews was a keen cricketer, and all the men in his family played for the North Down Cricket Club in Comber. They even donated the ground that is still used by the club to this day, and a trophy for the player of the year. He organised a game between North Down CC and Harland & Wolff CC, and he chose to play for his work's team, but the North Down bowlers got him out without scoring.

Steward Henry Etches was in charge of eight first-class portside cabins on B Deck, including that of Thomas Andrews at A36. Etches reported at the cabin of Mr Andrews every morning at 7am, describing how he used to be busy all the time working on his new ship. Apparently, Mr Andrews had charts rolled up by the side of his bed, and papers of all description on his desk, and he was constantly taking notes on any improvements that could be made. He would see him at other points during the days aboard, mainly on E Deck, and always with an entourage, taking notes for improvements.

Titanic dropped anchor at Roches Point outer anchorage in Queenstown and the officers welcomed aboard 123 more passengers. Some people disembarked, including an Irish priest named Father Francis Browne, and Kate Odell, who was travelling with her family. Father Browne had been gifted a new camera and a two-day cruise on *Titanic*. He had taken numerous photographs of life on the ship during its sailing to Cherbourg and then on to Queenstown. Father Browne had befriended an American couple who offered to pay his passage to New York, but on asking his superiors if he was allowed to accept, they considered his request to be narrow minded and replied sternly

'GET OFF THAT SHIP – PROVINCIAL'. Father Browne did as he was told, and his holy obedience probably saved his life.

As *Titanic* steamed her way out to sea from Queenstown, Eugene Daly of Westmeath played 'Elan's Lament' on his traditional Irish uilleann pipes. Fourth Officer Boxhall paused for thought when he noticed it was unusual that there were no sea birds flying around the ship as they usually did when they left a harbour. Chief Officer Henry Wilde (1872–1912) wrote a letter from Queenstown to his sister stating: 'I don't like this ship. I have a queer feeling about it.'

Victor and Maria 'Pepita' Penasco of Madrid were travelling with Maria's maid Fermina Ocana. They were listed as being of independent means, and Maria was the owner of a valuable collection of jewellery. They boarded at Cherbourg and travelled in first-class cabin C65, with Fermina in C109. Helen Bishop, who escaped in lifeboat 7, the first craft to leave the ship, said of them, 'Pepita and Victor were just like little canaries. They were so loving and were having such a lovely honeymoon that everyone on *Titanic* became interested in them.'

In fact, Victor was a nephew of Jose Canalejas, who was prime minister of Spain from 1910 to 1912, before being assassinated, and his mother Purificacion had warned them not to travel by boat because she believed that doing so while on honeymoon was bad luck. However, they had been in Paris when they saw a flyer advertising *Titanic's* maiden voyage and decided to extend their honeymoon and go to New York without Purificacion's knowledge.

Nothing of particular note seems to have happened during the first couple of days of the voyage, although the musicians were kept very busy. They were required to perform as two separate bands. One was a quintet of two violins, two cellos and a double base, which performed at teatime and for the occasional after-dinner concerts, and they had played at the service on the Sunday morning before the collision. There was also a trio consisting of a piano, a violin and a cello, which played in the à la carte restaurant and the Café Parisien. In all they had to learn the 350 tunes that appeared in the songbook handed out to first-class passengers.

A few suspicious eyes must have noticed one or two things that raised eyebrows and got their tongues wagging. They would have noticed that Mr and Mrs Marshall in second class did not really look suited to each other. She was a sheepish teenager with a broad Midlands accent, and he was a very business-like individual with a southern accent who must have been pushing 40. She was wearing a diamond-encrusted sapphire pendant that caught everyone's eye – just the type of thing an older man might buy for a young mistress, perhaps? They said they were on their way to California hoping the climate there would help him to get over a recent illness he had suffered, which was exactly the excuse he had given his family – including his wife and daughter.

In truth, his name was Henry Morley, a senior partner in his family's confectionary business in Worcester. Kate Phillips was an employee who worked in one of his sweet shops and they had begun a secret affair which developed in such a way that Henry was prepared to abandon his family and take Kate to re-settle on the west coast of America. Henry had the pendant made in Birmingham especially for Kate, and it was called L'Amour de la Mer – The Love of the Ocean.

Once they had made up their minds to act upon their feelings, Henry sold two of his shops and gave all the money to his wife and daughter for their security. Although the people around them must have had their suspicions, it is said that the only other person who knew about the affair was Henry's brother, who had actually agreed to drive them to Southampton, and is said to have waved them off.

Elizabeth Anne 'Lizzie' Wilkinson said she was on her way to spend her honeymoon in America. She boarded *Titanic* on a £26 joint ticket as a second-class passenger and was described as the new wife of Harry Bertram Faunthorpe, a businessman travelling to Philadelphia. They told others on the ship that they planned to honeymoon in California. However, Lizzie had a 'real' husband back in England.

Also in second class were Louis Hofmann and his two little boys known as 'Lolo', who was aged about 4, and his younger brother, who was known as Momon. However, their father was keeping a closely-guarded secret from the other passengers. His real name was Michel Navratil, and the boys were Michel Marcel and Edmond Roger. Michel had recently divorced from his wife, Marcelle, but she had gained custody over the children. During the Easter holidays he had absconded with them and intended to take them to America.

'Louis' led other passengers to believe that he was a widower, but they noticed that he was reluctant to get into conversation with anyone, especially concerning his two boys. He was very protective of them and never let them out of his sight. A French-speaking 17-year-old Swiss girl named Bertha Lehmann, who escaped in lifeboat 12, had stayed in her cabin every day suffering from sea-sickness, but after a few days she started to get used to the situation, and on feeling a little better she went up to the dining room to try to eat something. Louis and the boys were sat at the same table, and for some reason he felt he could trust her, and on being asked if he would like a game of cards, he asked Bertha to watch them for a while.

In later life Michel Marcel described the *Titanic* as: 'A magnificent ship! I remember looking down the length of the hull – the ship looked splendid. My brother and I played on the forward deck and were thrilled to be there. One morning my father, my brother and I were eating eggs in the second-class dining room. The sea was stunning. My feeling was one of total and utter well-being.'

Joseph Fynney was in his mid-thirties and was described as a 'handsome bachelor' with 'black hair, a smooth face, being a height of 5 feet 6 inches tall'. He often travelled to Montreal to visit his family, and it is likely that some of the crew who worked on various ships had noticed how strange it was that each time he made the trip, he had a young male companion with him. On this occasion it was an 18-year-old young man called Alfred Gaskell, who lived close to the church in Liverpool where Joe worked with delinquents. They shared a cabin on the same second-class ticket, and some passengers must have thought their situation was quite unusual to say the least.

Having a wife named Florette and three daughters back home in New York, 46-year-old Benjamin Guggenheim – 'The Copper King of New York' – had been living in Paris and had boarded at Cherbourg, along with his valet Victor Giglio, who was Liverpool-born, and his French driver René Pemot. Also in his party were a 24-year-old singer from Paris named Léontine Aubart, also known as 'Ninette', and her Swiss maid, Emma Saegesser. They all travelled in first class except René, who was in second class. Ben and Victor were in cabin B82, while Ninette and Emma were in B35. Mr Guggenheim had paid just over £163 for the three rooms. Emma stated in a radio interview that a woman had warned her 'a misfortune will happen for sure.' Apparently, she suffered a lot from seasickness and remained in her cabin for most of the voyage.

William Harbeck was a cinematographer, who had earned a good reputation for filming the aftermath of the 1906 San Francisco earthquake. He was not travelling on *Titanic* with his wife Catherine, but a 22-year-old model named Henriette Yvois whom he had met in Paris. According to Lawrence Beesley, William watched his 'wife' play solitaire throughout the voyage. William and Henrietta lost their lives in the sinking, and when William's body was recovered, it was found clutching a purse belonging to Henriette. When Catherine went to claim his body, she was almost turned away because they believed William's wife had died with him in the sinking. She later put in a claim for £5,000 for her husband's life, and £11,000 for the loss of 110,000 feet of moving picture films.

During the course of the voyage, seven individuals on board had formed what they referred to as 'Our Coterie'. This was based on a famous fashionable set of English aristocrats and intellectuals of the Edwardian period, known as 'The Coterie', which in turn had grown out of 'The Souls', an elite social group of the late Victorian period, which included many prominent political and intellectual figures. The members of *Titanic*'s Coterie were Colonel Archibald Gracie, who seems to have instigated the exclusive group, Helen Candee, James Clinch Smith, Hugh Woolner, Mauritz Stefansson, a Swedish man whose name was anglicised to Maurice Stephenson, Edward Colley and Edward Kent. Mr Smith, Mr Colley and Mr Kent lost their lives in the sinking.

As an example of the spirit of the group, Edward Colley is quoted as remarking,

> The dining room is low ceilinged but full of little tables for two, three and more in secluded corners. How I wish someone I liked was on board, but nice people don't sit at tables for two unless they are engaged or married. I wonder my blue blood didn't tell them that? They also have a restaurant where you can pay for meals if you get bored with the ordinary grub. Our most distinguished passengers seem to be W T Stead, Astor, oh, and the Countess of something, but her blood is only blue black (Give me good red corpuscles. I seem to know more about them).

On Friday, 12 April, as Mr Andrews was going in for dinner he was met by a fellow Belfast native in Nurse Stewardess Mary Sloan, and they started to chat. They talked of home, and how Mr Andrews' father and his wife were unwell. The nurse congratulated him on the beauty and perfection of the ship, to which he responded that the only part he did not like about *Titanic* was that it was taking them further away from home with every hour. His usual dinner companion, Dr William O'Loughlin, called to him hurry up or they might be late, but Mr Andrews was reluctant to go. Nurse Sloan noticed that he had, 'a very sad expression'.

Described as having 'grey-blue eyes, auburn hair, and spoke with an Irish accent', 24-year-old Stewardess Violet Jessop had transferred from *Olympic*. She was a devout Roman Catholic and always carried a rosary on her person, believing strongly in the power of prayer. She had brought on board a copy of a translated Hebrew prayer that an old Irish woman had given to her, which was supposed to protect her from fire and water. Her room-mate was a 50-year-old Liverpudlian named Elizabeth Leather, who was married to an Eccles veterinary surgeon. She had previously served on board RMS *Cedric*, along with Mary Gregson and Sarah Stap, who had also transferred to *Titanic* for her maiden voyage.

Jessop had become friends with Jock Hume, the band's Scottish violinist, and it was a habit of hers to have a walk on deck to get some fresh air before she retired for the night. On the Saturday evening, 13 April, as she walked leisurely along, she thought to herself: 'If the sun did fail to shine so brightly on the fourth day out, and if the little nip crept into the air as evening set in, it only served to emphasise the warmth and luxuriousness within.'

New Yorkers Elizabeth Lines and her teenage daughter Mary had been living in Paris, and were travelling to the United States to attend Elizabeth's son's graduation from Dartmouth College. They occupied cabin D28. On Saturday, 13 April, the two ladies finished lunch in the first-class dining room on D Deck, and then continued their habit of stopping for coffee in the adjoining reception room. Captain Smith and Bruce Ismay, who Mary recognised from living in New York, came and sat at a table close to them, and they began to discuss the possibility of having the last boilers lit. Could this have been because of their desire to make the ship go faster?

On the same day, Walter and Mahala Douglas were taking a stroll along the boat deck. They were from Cedar Rapids, Idaho, and were travelling in cabin C86. Mrs Douglas had a maid named Berthe Leroy, who was also on the ship. As they strolled along, they came upon a member of the crew who was dangling a bucket on a rope over the side of the ship; the reason being to take a sample to test the temperature of the water. The couple noticed that the bucket had not reached the water when he hauled it back up again. To their surprise, he took the empty bucket over to a hose pipe lying on the deck, filled it and tested the temperature with a thermometer. Mrs Douglas suggested that they should report what they had witnessed, but Walter dismissed it as not being important enough. However, Mrs Douglas remained concerned because she and several of their fellow passengers were aware that icebergs had been reported in the region. After dining in the à la carte restaurant and on the way back to their stateroom, they remarked to each other how the ship seemed to be going much faster than they had experienced during the course of the voyage, with the vibration, especially near the stairwells, feeling more pronounced than usual.

Charles and Annie Stengel were New Yorkers, and Charles had a German father, with whom he had worked in the industry of leather manufacturing. They were in stateroom C116, which was near the engines. Because of the location of their cabin, they became aware that the ship was going faster every day. Mr Stengel placed a wager with some other first-class passengers as to who could estimate the closest to the headway the liner was making. It was calculated that the ship made 546 knots. Mr Stengel would need to be careful when it came to his betting as there were three men with notorious reputations for being tricksters and card sharps among the first-class passengers.

There were good sports facilities on *Titanic*, which were exclusively for first-class passengers. The gymnasium was situated near the forward grand staircase, along the starboard side of the boat deck. It was a bright room lit by natural light and equipped with state-of-the-art exercise equipment, including two electric camels, an electric horse, a rowing machine, punching bag, a weightlifting machine and mechanical bicycles. There was also a permanent physical educator on staff named Thomas McCawley, who assisted passengers in using the devices. The gymnasium was segregated by gender and age.

There featured a squash/racquet court in the bow of G Deck. It measured 30 feet long by 20 feet wide and had its own instructor on staff named Frederick Wright. There was a spectator's gallery on F Deck overlooking the court. It could be entered only by a separate staircase starting on D Deck, from where a passenger would descend the three decks past the viewing platform to G Deck. The charge to play was 2 shillings or 50 cents for half an hour.

There was a heated swimming pool on F Deck measuring 30 feet by 14 feet, although it was comparatively small and was usually referred to as a 'bath'. The water depth was 5 feet 4 inches at the deep end and 4 feet 6 inches at the shallow end. Heated salt water from a tank and cold sea water were pumped into the pool once the ship was out at sea. The room offered thirteen changing cubicles and two shower stalls for convenience. The pool cost 1 shilling or 50 cents to use but was open to men free of charge between 6 and 8 am, for early morning exercise. The attendant who looked after the facility was Isaac Widgery, from Bristol, who used the name James. He received £3 15s a month in wages.

Of the many keen sportsmen on board, it is likely that Charles Williams would have used the squash court, as he was a successful racquets player. He had won the English Open title in 1911, and the World Championship early in 1912; he was on his way to defend his title in New York. Peter Sloan, the chief electrician, was a championship-winning swimmer, and two young men with Welsh accents from third class named Dai Bowen and Leslie Williams would have made use of the gym. They were considered to be highly promising boxers who were on their way to the United States for a series of boxing contests. They did not complete their journey.

Colonel Archibald Gracie IV, late of the Seventh New York Militia, stayed in first-class cabin C51, and, having decided that he had neglected his health recently, he wanted to spend some of the Saturday morning doing physical exercise on the squash courts and in the swimming pool, so he booked in with Frederick Wright, the squash court attendant. He attended church services, had an early lunch, and spent the rest of the day reading and socialising. He intended to go to bed early that night so he could continue with his exercise regime on the squash courts on the following day. The squash court attendant earned £1 a week wages and probably had to rely on tips from his clientele.

He had spent his time during the voyage in accompanying several middle-aged women. They included three former Lamson sisters, whose married names were Charlotte Appleton, Malvina Cornell and Caroline Brown. They were accompanied by Edith Corse Evans, who is believed to have been related to the sisters. They had been in Paris for the funeral of another sister named Elizabeth, who had passed away on 25 March, and who was married to Sir Victor Drummond. The sisters were not aware that their aunt and uncle, Charles and Josephine Marshall, were also on board the ship.

Many passengers took regular strolls along the promenades after dinner. It is likely that some of them became aware that there did not seem to be enough lifeboats for the vast number of people on board the ship and they expressed concern at what would happen if there was a reason to have to evacuate. But they were consoled by the fact that they were on board the unsinkable *Titanic*.

On Saturday afternoon, 13 April, George Widener and his wife, Eleanor, were standing on the first-class promenade deck talking to Bruce Ismay, when Captain Smith came walking by as he was making his way towards the back of the ship. Without a word, he passed a telegram to Mr Ismay. It was the one received from *Baltic* at 1:42pm, which Ismay put in his pocket and walked away. Marian Thayer and Emily Ryerson also met Mr Ismay on the promenade deck, and he showed them the telegram. Arthur and Emily Ryerson were accompanied by their daughters Suzette and Emily, and their 13-year-old son, John Borie. Arthur was one of the richest men on the ship.

After doing his rounds on Sunday, 14 April, Mr Andrews was of the opinion that all was shipshape and Bristol fashion: 'Today I made my usual inspection of the ship. I talked to a few people on the deck and then went around the ship to see if there was anyone who could use a little help... No problems of great importance have risen so far. As passengers are starting to get comfortable in the ship there has been less for me to do. So far, it's been a delightful cruise for everyone.'

One of twins, Harvey Collyer, along with his wife Charlotte, known as 'Lottie', were travelling with their 8-year-old daughter, Marjorie, known as 'Madge', destined for Idaho in the United States, where Harvey had bought some land for fruit farming; and they also believed that the new air might help ease Lottie's tuberculosis. A grocer by profession, and a member of the bell-ringers at their local church in Basingstoke, Harvey had received a long peel of bells to mark the family's departure to America, and on the morning of *Titanic's* departure, he withdrew all their savings in cash from the Southampton branch of their bank.

Lottie stated:

> ...on Sunday, April 14 I was up and about. At dinner time I was at my place in the saloon and enjoyed the meal, though I thought it too heavy and rich. No effort had been spared to give even the second cabin passengers on that Sunday the best dinner that money could buy. After I had eaten, I listened to the orchestra for a little while, and then at nine o'clock or half-past-nine I went to my cabin. I had just climbed into my berth when a stewardess came in. She was a sweet woman who had been very kind to me. I take this opportunity to thank her for I shall never see her again. She went down with the *Titanic.*
>
> 'Do you know where we are?' she said pleasantly, 'we are in what is called the Devil's Hole.'
>
> 'What does that mean?' I asked.
>
> 'That is a dangerous part of the Ocean,' she answered. 'Many accidents have happened near there. They say that icebergs drift down as far as this. It's getting to be very cold on deck so perhaps there is ice around us now.'
>
> She left the cabin and I soon dropped off to sleep. Her talk about icebergs had not frightened me, but it shows that the crew were awake to the danger.

Married couples and families with children in first- and second-class cabins were allowed to stay together, but in third class all male and female passengers were separated in different cabins. The men and older sons had to sleep in cabins at the front of the ship, while women, older daughters and young children had to stay in accommodation at the stern. In the third-class family cabins a few people had begun to make friends.

Lawrence Beesley reported: 'I often noticed how the third-class passengers were enjoying every minute of the time. A most uproarious skipping game of the mixed-doubles type was the great favourite, while in and out and roundabout went a Scotsman with his bagpipes.' This was probably Eugene Daly on his traditional Irish uilleann pipes.

Among the third-class passengers were Rhoda Abbott, who was travelling with her two teenage sons, Rossmore and Eugene. She had been married to the London-born ex-United States Middleweight Boxing Champion, Stanton Abbott.

Elizabeth Dowdell was the nursemaid to 6-year-old Virginia Emanuel, in the employ of her mother Estelle, an opera singer. All three had travelled across the Atlantic to London, where Estelle had gained for herself a six-month contract to appear in London theatres. Elizabeth and Virginia boarded *Titanic* as third-class passengers, and they shared a cabin with Amy Stanley.

Frank and Emily Goldsmith and their 9-year-old son Frankie were moving to Detroit to join family who were already established there. They had lost a son in the previous year. Also Detroit-bound was Thomas Theobald and Alfred Rush. Alfred was aged just 17 and was in the care of the Goldsmiths, who were friends of his parents. He was on his way to start a new life in America, where his older brother Charles had settled. Also in the care of the Goldsmiths was May Howard, an East Anglian laundry worker who was on her way to New York to work as a nanny. She suffered several bouts of seasickness during the voyage.

Arthur Gee had apparently organised the trip across the Atlantic to take a job as manager of a linen mill near Mexico City, after which he was contemplating retiring. His first-class ticket cost him nearly £40. He intended to sail from Liverpool, but because industrial unrest had affected the port there, the ship was delayed and, as fate would have it, he happily agreed to travel to Southampton to board the brand new luxury liner RMS *Titanic*.

His dog had acted strangely on the day he made his way to the station, as if it sensed foreboding and was trying to warn him not to get on the train. His local newspaper in Lancashire later reported:

> He kept a dog, which usually reserved its most affectionate demonstrations for Mr Gee's children. Mr Gee, in the course of his business, made frequent journeys from home, but his going and comings were apparently regarded with unconcern by the dog. On the occasion of his departure to embark at Southampton, however, the dog followed the cab to the railway station, and at the station jumped about Mr Gee in so demonstrative a fashion that he remarked on the strangeness of the incident to a friend who was seeing him off, and said how remarkable it was that the dog should appear to know that he was going on a long voyage.

Esther Hart, her husband, Benjamin, and their 7-year-old daughter Eva, were on their way to Canada, where Ben intended to set up as a builder. Esther described Eva as being 'very bonny', and that 'everybody takes notice of her ... the teddy bear.' Esther had never had any kind of premonitions before, but she considered all the talk of the ship being unsinkable was flying in the face of God, and she stated: 'I can honestly say that from the moment the journey to Canada was mentioned till the time we got aboard *Titanic,* I never contemplated with any other feelings but those of dread and uneasiness.'

She had no faith in the ship no matter how big and fancy it was. Her forebodings caused her to be particularly wary of how the ship was performing, and she was not convinced when she had been told that it was so big that it was not supposed to roll badly as it pounded through the waves. She slept during the day and stayed awake at night, seemingly presuming if there was going to be a problem it would happen during the dark hours. She wrote:

> Anyhow it rolls enough for me, I shall never forget it. It is nice weather but awfully windy and cold. They say we may get into New York Tuesday night but we were really due early on Wednesday morning. The sailors say we have had a wonderful passage, up to now there has been no tempest, but God knows what it must be like when there is one. This rough expanse of water, no land in sight and the ship rolling from side to side is very wonderful though they say this ship does not roll on account of its size. We have met some nice people on board and so it has been nice so far. But oh the long, long days and nights it's the longest week I ever spent in my life.

Esther had been feeling sick all Saturday and did not eat or drink, but she had got over it by Sunday morning and she and Eva attended morning service. Eva sang the popular hymn 'Oh Lord Our Help in Ages Past'. Esther said: 'That is the hymn she sang so nicely, so she sang out loud.' Esther wrote that as a treat: 'She [Eva] has had a nice ball and a box of toffee and a photo of this ship bought her today.' After lunch they met Ben in the library, where Esther and Eva wrote a letter intended for her mother. The sea must have been a bit unsettled at the time as Esther pointed out: 'You see the letter all of a screw is when she rolls and shakes my arm.'

It was known that there were some farm animals on board the ship, and earlier that day Ellen 'Nellie' Hocking and her Cornish family had been sitting out on the second-class promenade deck when suddenly they heard a rooster crow. Mrs Hocking had already expressed unease about the ship and remembered an old superstition that a cock crowing at night was a warning of disaster. It prompted her to remark, 'I don't like that. I think something is going to happen.'

Charles Melville Hays – 'The Railway King' – looked at it more realistically, and he is reported to have made remarks criticising the way the steamship lines were competing to win passengers with ever-faster vessels. He is said to have commented, 'The time will come soon when this trend will be checked by some appalling disaster.'

Reverend Ernest Carter of Whitechapel in London was travelling with his wife Lillian for a break in America. Lillian's father was Thomas Hughes, the author of *Tom Brown's School Days*, which he had based on his experiences in the school in the 1830s.

On the early Sunday evening, Reverend Carter presided over a service of hymns for a hundred or so passengers in the second-class dining saloon. Marion Wright led the singing, accompanied on the piano by Douglas Norman, in which she sang solos of 'Lead Kindly Light: Amid the Encircling Gloom' and 'There is a Green Hill Far Away'. Reverend Carter preceded each item with a history of the hymn and its author, in which he would have stated that the former was written by Cardinal Newman, and was often sung during times of stress, and the latter hymn was penned by the Irish writer Cecil Frances Alexander, who also wrote 'All Things Bright and Beautiful' and the Christmas carol 'Once in Royal David's City'.

At about 10pm the steward arrived to set out the tables for breakfast and Carter brought the proceedings to a close by thanking the purser and adding how everyone was looking forward to their arrival in New York. Apparently, his closing words were: 'It is the first time that there have been hymns sung on this boat on a Sunday evening, but we trust and pray that it won't be the last.'

George Widener was a wealthy tramcar manufacturer from Philadelphia, who had been staying at the Ritz Hotel in Paris with his wife, his son, Harry, his servant Edwin Keeping, who came from London, and his wife's German maid, Amalie Gieger. They had travelled to England on RMS *Mauretania* to ensure the safe arrival of thirty silver plates once owned by Nell Gwyn, which were being donated to the London Museum. They subsequently arrived in Paris to purchase a wedding dress for the upcoming wedding of their daughter Eleanor.

On the evening of the disaster, the Wideners hosted a dinner party in the à la carte restaurant in honour of Captain Smith. The guests included Mr and Mrs Thayer, Major Archibald Butt, Clarence Moore, and Mr and Mrs William Carter.

Saloon Steward Tom Whiteley remembered:

> Orders had been issued Sunday to make the dinner the finest ever served on a ship, regardless of expense, and the orders were carried out. The one topic of conversation was the new boat and the speed she was making… At one time Doctor O'Loughlin stood up, and, raising a glass of champagne, cried, 'Let us drink to the mighty *Titanic.*' With cries of approval, everybody drank to the toast. I believe it was generally thought by all of those at the tables that the *Titanic* would reach New York late Tuesday or early Wednesday morning, and the captain and other officers were planning a big banquet after the landing in anticipation of the trip record breaker. The dinner broke up shortly before 9 o'clock, and the men retired to the smoking rooms, while some of the women went to their staterooms, and others strolled along the promenade.

The senior operator in control of the Marconi wireless was Jack Phillips, who had just celebrated his 25th birthday on the ship two days earlier, while his assistant Harold Bride was only 22, although he looked even younger than that. They were receiving messages from other ships concerning ice in the area. They had been informed by Captain Smith that icebergs were usually present more to the north of their position, but at 9am they received a message from Cunard's RMS *Coronia* stating that they had seen: 'Bergs, growlers and field ice.' This was followed at 11:40am by a warning from SS *Noordam,* which was also on its way to New York, simply stating that they had seen: 'Much ice.' At 1:42pm RMS *Baltic* warned of: 'Icebergs, and large quantities of field ice.' At 7:30pm Harold overheard a transmission from SS *Californian* to its fellow Leyland Line ship the SS *Antillian,* stating that they had seen: 'Three large bergs five miles to the southward of us.'

Harold was concerned for Jack Phillips and the overload of work he had to deal with.

> 'I remember how tired he [Phillips] was and got out of bed to relieve him. I didn't even feel the shock. I hardly knew it had happened until after the captain had come to us. There was no jolt whatsoever. I was standing by Phillips telling him to go to bed when the captain put his head into the cabin.
>
> 'We've struck an iceberg,' the captain said, 'and I'm having an inspection made to tell what it has done for us. You better get ready to send out a call for assistance. But don't send it until I tell you.'
>
> The captain went away, and in ten minutes, I should estimate the time, he came back. We could hear a terrible confusion outside, but there was

not the least thing to indicate that there was any trouble. The wireless was working perfectly.

'Send the call for assistance,' said the captain, barely putting his head in the door.

'What call should I send?' asked Phillips.

'The regulation international call for help, just that,' the captain replied, and then he was gone again.

Phillips began to send 'C Q D' – he flashed away at it and we were joking while he did so. All of us made light of the disaster. We joked that way while he flashed signals for about five minutes. Then the captain came back.

'What are you sending?' he asked.

'C Q D' Phillips replied.

The humour of the situation appealed to me. I cut in with a little remark that made us all laugh, including the captain.

'Send S O S', I said, 'It's the new call, and it may be your last chance to send it.'

Phillips, with a laugh, changed the signal to 'S O S.'

The captain told us we had been struck amidships, or just aft of amidships. It was ten minutes, Phillips told me, after he noticed the iceberg, but the slight jolt was the only signal to us that a collision had occurred. We thought we were a good distance away. We said lots of funny things to each other in the next few minutes. We picked up the first steamship *Frankfurt*; gave her our position and said we had struck an iceberg and needed assistance.

The *Frankfurt* operator went away to tell his captain. He came back, and we told him we were sinking by the head, and that we could observe a distinct list forward.

The *Carpathia* answered our signal, and we told her our position, and said we are sinking by the head. The operator went to tell the captain, and in five minutes returned, and told us the *Carpathia* was putting about and heading for us.

Our captain had left us at this time, and Phillips told me to run and tell him what the *Carpathia* had answered. I did so, and I went through an awful mass of people to his cabin [the wheelhouse]. The decks were full of scrambling men and women.

I came back and heard Phillips giving the *Carpathia* further directions. Phillips told me to put on my clothes. Until that moment I forgot I wasn't dressed. I went to my cabin and dressed. I brought an overcoat to Phillips, and as it was very cold I slipped the overcoat upon him while he worked.

Every few minutes Phillips would send me to the captain with little messages. They were merely telling how *Carpathia* was coming our way and giving her speed.

STARBOARD FRONT

LIFEBOAT 7

After the collision, it became difficult for anyone to be heard because there was a tremendous roar as the ship's exhausts let off steam, and they had to use hand signals to pass on messages. The noise carried on for quite some time before it stopped abruptly.

Fifth Officer Harold Lowe (1882–1944) remembered that when he reached the boat deck: 'I could feel by my feet there was something wrong – it is not listing it is tipping – she was by the bow; she was very much by the bow. She had a grade downhill... by the head.'

Fifth Officer Lowe was a 29-year-old single man from north-west Wales. He had joined the White Star Line only fifteen months prior to boarding RMS *Titanic,* and this was to be his first transatlantic crossing. Fireman Thomas Threlfall considered him to be 'A gentleman and a Britisher', and a female passenger described him as 'A leader with a cool head, desperate courage, and a knowledge of the sea.'

Lifeboat 7 was situated at the front of the ship on the starboard side, which happened to be the area above where the ship had hit the iceberg. It was the first to be launched at about 12:40am, or just after, supervised by First Officer Murdoch and Fifth Officer Lowe. Lookouts Archie Jewell and George Hogg were placed in charge, and Able Seaman William Weller was the only other crew member in the boat. All three were members of the deck crew, the majority of whom escaped in the lifeboats; all six of the lookouts escaped. There are believed to have been about forty-two passengers in lifeboat 7, all of them being first class, and many of them had been playing cards when the collision occurred.

First Officer Murdoch was a married Scotsman who had joined the White Star Line in 1900 and the Royal Naval Reserve in 1902. He had served aboard RMS *Olympic* since May 1911, and was on that ship when she collided with HMS *Hawke*. Charlotte Collyer, a surviving passenger, said of him: 'He was a masterful man, astoundingly brave and cool... and thought him a bull-dog of a man who would not be afraid of anything.'

George Hogg was one of several people on the ship who were associated with Kingston-upon-Hull, and while the emergency was being assessed, he and Lookout Alfred Evans had relieved Fred Fleet and Reg Lee in the crow's nest. However, realising the situation was serious when they saw people running about with lifebelts on, they climbed down and went to the boat deck to see how they could help. Hogg was asked by a boatswain to go and a get a Jacob's ladder (a flexible ladder with metal or wooden rungs between two lengths of sturdy rope), but when he got back, First Officer Murdoch ordered him to get into lifeboat 7 to check if the plugs were in, and on finding that they were secure, he got back out onto the deck. First Officer Murdoch then ordered him back in to help get the passengers on board, and for him to stay on board to help with the rowing.

Dorothy Gibson, Frederic Seward and William Sloper, had, as Dorothy put it 'spent a pleasant Sunday evening playing bridge with a couple of friendly New York bankers.' Dorothy was an actor, who was travelling with her mother, Pauline; Frederic was a New York lawyer, and William was a stockbroker, who, it seems, should have sailed back to America on the *Mauretania,* but changed ships after he had met and grown fond of a woman named Alice Fortune, while she was on vacation in Europe with her family, and bought tickets for *Titanic* instead.

Despite a request by the library steward for them to finish their card game so he could put out the lights and retire, the players carried on, until Dorothy felt 'a long drawn, sickening crunch', and while not particularly alarmed, she decided to investigate. Quickly noticing that the deck was 'lopsided', she rushed to her room to fetch her mother, and they went straight to the boat deck. Because it was so quiet there at the then early stages of the emergency, when Chief Officer Murdoch offered her a place in lifeboat 7, she asked if her bridge partners Fred Seward and William Sloper could join them, and they were allowed.

Mr Sloper pointed out that many people on board felt that *Titanic* was unsinkable, and therefore did not want to leave the well-lit deck to set off into the dark waters in small boats. He was later accused by a New York reporter of having dressed as a woman to escape the ship, but this was probably a deliberately made-up slant against his name as he was a man who had survived the sinking. He left before the 'women and children first' rule had been fully established.

At the time of the disaster Dorothy Gibson was having an affair with Jules Brulatour, co-founder of Universal Studios. Soon after the sinking she became involved in the production of a short silent film entitled *Saved from the Titanic*, in which she starred, and to enhance the authenticity of film, she wore the same clothes she had worn on the night of the disaster. It was released on 16 May 1912 and received some positive reviews, though some people thought it was in bad taste to be released as a commercial venture so soon after the tragic event.

The crew did everything they could to try to persuade the passengers to enter the craft, but they would not. Eventually, an American businessman named Dickinson Bishop and his second wife Helen were persuaded to get in. Others then followed.

The Bishops had been on a four-month honeymoon around Europe and North Africa, during which time Helen had become pregnant, and they had acquired a dog which they named 'Freu Freu'. They were in their stateroom when the ship struck the iceberg, and Dickinson went on deck to investigate, only to be told the same as other passengers that there was nothing to worry about. However, a fellow passenger named Albert Stewart convinced them of the danger, and they returned to the boat deck. Still thinking that it was probably nothing too serious, they left their dog behind. When they arrived on deck, they were told to get into lifeboat 7. Dickinson was also later falsely accused as dressing as a woman to get into a lifeboat, probably for the same reason as the slant against William Sloper.

As the lifeboat was being rowed away from the stricken ship, quite nonchalantly, Helen Bishop suddenly remarked, 'We have to be rescued for the rest of my prophecy to come true.' The reason for the remark was that while she and her new husband were in Egypt, she decided to visit a fortune teller. The seer divined her future, saying that she would survive a shipwreck, and an earthquake, before an automobile accident would end her life. Helen was pregnant at the time of the sinking, but she lost the baby, who they had named Randall Walton, only two days into its life – something the fortune teller appears to have failed to detect.

Although it is not certain in which lifeboat Scottish-born Mary Marvin (formerly Farquharson) left the stricken ship, she and her new husband, New Yorker Daniel Marvin, were returning to America after spending three months in Europe on their honeymoon. The marriage of the two teenagers had been the first ever to be filmed (cinematographed) and Daniel was an associate of the inventor, Thomas Edison. It seems they had married just in time as Mary was three months pregnant when she boarded the ship. Daniel accompanied his new wife from their D30 cabin to one of the lifeboats, remarking, 'It's alright, little girl. You go. I will stay.' He blew her a kiss as the lifeboat was lowered. Mary collapsed on board *Carpathia* when she realised that her new husband was lost. A daughter named Mary (known as Peggy) was born on 21 October 1912.

About twenty-six couples were either on their way back from spending their honeymoon in Europe, or on the way to spend their honeymoon in America, and another honeymoon couple who got into the first lifeboat was John Snyder, an American businessman who was travelling back from Europe with his new wife, Nellie.

Three Frenchmen named Pierre Maréchal, Paul Chevré, and Alfred Omont, as well as an American named Lucian Smith, were playing bridge in the Café Parisien when all four felt a slight shock as the ship collided with the iceberg. However, they thought that it had been caused by a wave.

Pierre was a French film producer and aviator, and father of racing driver Jean-Pierre Maréchal. Paul was a sculptor who had won a bronze medal when the Olympic Games were held as part of the Paris Exposition of 1900. Alfred Omont was a cotton dealer, and Lucian Smith was on his honeymoon.

Pierre went out of the café to investigate, where he came upon a few other inquiring passengers, who were not showing any sense of alarm. He could see nothing amiss, so he went back to the card game.

Paul considered it too cold to go outside to investigate, so asked a steward to open a porthole and have a look. The steward simply reported that it was a clear night. However, they heard the sound of hurrying feet on the decks above and shouting that was getting louder and seemed more serious, so they all pocketed their cards and went out on deck.

While they waited on the boat deck for some confirmation of the situation so that they could get back to their game, Captain Smith, apparently chewing a toothpick, came down from the Bridge and said, 'You had better put your life preservers on, as a precaution.'

As the lifeboat was being occupied, First Officer Murdoch asked Alfred Omont if he wanted to get in. Some of the passengers shouted for him not to do so as they had such confidence in the ship. However, he saw that the sea was calm, so he decided to 'jump into the boat and see what would happen.' Pierre Maréchal and Paul Chevré joined him.

Lily Potter, with her daughter Olive Earnshaw, along with Margaret Hays and her Pomeranian dog named 'Bebe', had been touring Europe and had boarded at Cherbourg. They were all in bed when they felt the ship's engines stop, so Olive and Margaret went to Lily's room, and Lily asked them to go and see what the trouble was. On their return they reported: 'We have hit an iceberg, but the steward told us we should not worry and should go back to bed.'

However, Lily was a little unnerved, so they got dressed and wrapped Bebe in a blanket. On their way to the boat deck, they met Gilbert Tucker standing on the landing of C Deck waiting for advice. He had been an admirer of Margaret's for quite some time in Europe and was staying in the next cabin to theirs on E Deck. He helped them to put on lifejackets, and then all four of them and the dog went up onto the boat deck. As they stood on the starboard side of the vessel, another passenger named James Clinch Smith, who had 'showed no sign of fear' walked by and jokingly commented, 'Oh, I suppose we ought to put a life preserver on the little doggie, too.' Clinch Smith was later noted for his bravery, but he did not survive.

When the call was heard for women to get into lifeboat 7, Gilbert remembered that there was some hesitancy at first, as many 'preferred the vast bulk of the *Titanic*, supposed to be the staunchest ever built, to the frail and pitifully-small looking lifeboats.'

Eventually, Lily stepped in, followed by Olive and Margaret – and Bebe the dog – leaving Gilbert behind. However, the vessel was far from full, so when it had descended about 15 feet, those on board called up to Gilbert and a couple of other men to come along, so they slid down the painters (ropes) and got in; Gilbert suggesting that they would be back on board by breakfast.

Baron Alfred von Drachstedt, William Greenfield and Henry Blank were playing cards together in the first-class smoking room when the collision occurred. The baron was actually Alfred Nourney, a German 'gentleman'; William was a furrier from New York who was travelling with his mother, Blanche; and Henry was a jeweller.

Henry remembered feeling 'a slight jar', so they stopped their game and went to the promenade deck to try to spot the berg, and on their return the ship came to a stop. Puzzled by that, they decided to go to F Deck and were alarmed when they saw that sea water, deep enough to cover their shoes, was flowing into the squash court. They immediately went to their rooms to prepare for a possible evacuation of the liner. Henry was one of the first to arrive on the starboard side of the boat deck, followed by Alfred Nourney, the Greenfields, and Prussia-born Antoinette Flegenheim, a wealthy New York socialite and friend of the Greenfields. They all got into lifeboat 7.

Irish-born James McGough was a Philadelphia department store buyer, who shared a cabin with John Flynn. After the collision he left his stateroom on the starboard side of the ship and was told by a steward named George Dodd that there was no danger and that they should go back to bed. However, James was in no doubt that the rumbling and quivering was caused by an iceberg, as his room had been too hot and his porthole was consequently open, so as the berg swept by, chunks of ice fell through the porthole and into his cabin. After alerting the female passengers across the passage from his room, he, along with Flynn, went up to the promenade deck. There they were ordered to put on lifebelts. They returned to their cabin to get their belts, and on returning to the boat deck they saw women and children being put into lifeboats. As there was great hesitation on the part of the passengers to get into the boats, a large officer gave McGough a push into lifeboat 7, saying: 'You are a big fellow, get into the boat.'

Catherine Crosby and her daughter Harriet also got into lifeboat 7. They were travelling with her husband, Captain Edward Crosby, an American Civil War veteran, who had founded the Crosby Transportation Company, which operated four steamers out of Milwaukee. They had been awakened by what Catherine described as a 'thumping of the boat', and 'the engines stopped suddenly.' After a while Edward got dressed and went to find out what was happening. When he came back, he said to Catherine, rather bluntly, 'You will lie there and drown!' He then went to his daughter's cabin and informed her that the ship was badly damaged, 'but I think the water-tight compartments will hold her up.' He went off again and Catherine stated: 'My husband did not come back again after he left me and I don't know what became of him, except that his body was found and brought back to Milwaukee for burial.'

Mrs Crosby stated: 'There were absolutely no lights in the lifeboats, and they did not even know whether the plug was in the bottom of the boat to prevent the boat from sinking; there were no lanterns, no provisions, and no lights, nothing at all in these boats but the oars. One of the officers asked one of the passengers for a watch with which to light up the bottom of the boat to see if the plug was in place.'

Most of the equipment for the lifeboats was kept locked away in a cupboard on deck for fear of them being stolen, but in the rush most of the items were left behind. The hole caused icy cold water to rush in. Luckily, as Dorothy Gibson explained, 'This was remedied by voluntary contributions from the lingerie of the women and garments of the men.' However, they still had to sit for hours with their feet soaking in icy cold water.

As they drifted on the waves, Alfred Omont took time to assess the situation. In his opinion the boat could not have held more than thirty in safety, and he considered the idea of putting sixty people in a lifeboat of its size as ridiculous. Lifeboats 7 and 5 are believed to have been the first regular lifeboats to reach *Carpathia*, probably at about 6am.

LIFEBOAT 5

Lifeboat number 5 was the second to be launched, at 12:45am. It was prepared by Third Officer Pitman, who was joined by First Officer Murdoch and Fifth Officer Lowe, after they had launched lifeboat 7. This lifeboat was also filled with first-class passengers, including eight married couples. Third Officer Pitman was in charge, along with Quartermaster Alfred Olliver; Fireman Alfred Shiers; Henry Etches, a first-class bedroom steward to some of the rich people on the ship; Southampton-born Elgar Guy, an assistant boot steward; and two married first-class stewardesses named Mabel Bennett and Hypatia McLaren.

Third Officer Pitman was the 35-year-old unmarried son of a West Country farmer. After serving on several ships with other companies, he had moved to the White Star Line in 1906, and had recently served as second officer on RMS *Oceanic II*. He is known to have suffered from seasickness. He had heard a noise and thought the ship was coming to anchor. After a few minutes he decided to go on deck and look around just outside the officers' quarters, where he did not see or hear anything unusual. He went back inside where he met Second Officer Lightoller, who told him they had 'evidently' hit something. Nevertheless, Third Officer Pitman went back to his bunk, but after a few minutes he got back up, 'as it was no use trying to go to sleep again, as I was due on watch in a few minutes.' While he was putting on his coat, Fourth Officer Boxhall came in and informed him that the mail room was flooded. He asked Fourth Officer Boxhall what they had hit, and he said an iceberg. After that he put his coat on and went on deck, leaving behind his discharge book and a 'comprehensive collection of stamps'. On deck he saw men uncovering the lifeboats on the portside of the ship, and he met Officer Moody on the after part of the deck, and: 'I asked him if he had seen the iceberg; he answered, No, but there was ice on the forward well deck.' He then saw 'a whole bunch' of firemen coming up from the starboard side of the ship.

Second Officer Lightoller, known as 'Lights', had served under Captain Smith on previous ships. The son of an army captain, he was a member of a family who were prominent in the Lancashire cotton trade. He had suffered several domestic tragedies in his early life, which had resulted in the death of his mother and three siblings. He was involved in three other perilous maritime incidents, which resulted in several encounters in shark-infested waters – and with scavenging albatross-infested skies. He was shipwrecked and faced near starvation on one of the remotest islands on Earth. He was caught up in a cyclone and nearly drowned off the coast of West Africa, and he almost died of malaria. He suffered a year of a harsh Canadian winter during the 1898 Klondike gold rush. He came back penniless, although the banjo he played to keep up spirits survived intact. He joined the White Star Line in 1900, and the Royal Naval Reserve in the following year.

Fourth Officer Boxhall was an unmarried man who had joined the White Star Line in September 1907 and had been confirmed as sub-lieutenant in the Royal Naval Reserve as recently as 1 October 1911. He had served on other liners and was a month before his 28th birthday. Like Bert Pitman, he suffered from seasickness.

Harry Eches was off duty when the collision occurred. On hearing some commotion, he became curious and walked down E Deck and along the alleyway known as Scotland Road. As he entered the third-class accommodation, he came upon a passenger carrying a lump of ice who must have tried in vain to get others to believe that the ship had hit an iceberg and was in danger. He dropped the ice to the floor and exclaimed: 'Will you believe me now?' Harry took the hint and went along the corridors trying to stir the passengers into action. He banged on the door of cabin C78, and when the people inside asked what the trouble was, Harry explained. Yet despite his warnings, the occupants did not open the door, so he moved on.

On returning to his station, he spent his time trying to get the first-class passengers to put on their lifebelts. Ben Guggenheim protested saying: 'This will hurt!' and only agreed to wear his after a great deal of persuasion. Harry gave the tycoon a thick sweater to wear before leading him out onto the boat deck. However, Mr Guggenheim soon returned to his cabin to put on his best velvet evening wear, and his friends did the same. He later stated to fellow passengers: 'We've dressed up in our best and are prepared to go down like gentlemen.'

Fourth Officer Boxhall went along the length of the starboard side of one of the lower decks to try to provide a damage assessment, but he could not see any. However, on C Deck he came upon a man who was carrying a lump of ice, and he took it from him. He returned to the Bridge and reported that he had not seen any actual damage to the ship. His next mission was to find a carpenter, who told him that the ship was taking on water fast, and a man from the mail room also stated that there was water in the ship's hold. On reaching the mail room, Fourth Officer Boxhall was alarmed to discover that the water: 'was rising rapidly up the ladder and I could hear it rushing in.' He saw mailbags floating around in the water. He reported what he had seen to the men on the Bridge, and then he went to the officers' quarters to warn the men who were off-duty. Then he heard the disturbing order that they should get the lifeboats ready, so he went up and down the boat deck on both sides of the ship to help with the unlacing and initial preparation of the lifeboats.

Bruce Ismay 'with his dressing gown and pyjamas on' was also at the scene, and he shouted to Third Officer Pitman to 'Hurry up; there is no time to waste! Fill the boat with women and children!' To which Pitman, not knowing who he was, replied that he would await the captain's orders first. It eventually dawned on him who Ismay was, so Pitman went to the Bridge and told the captain what he had suggested, and the captain told him to 'Carry on' – meaning to 'go ahead' with the suggestion.

On returning to lifeboat 5, Third Officer Pitman and Bruce Ismay helped several women and at least two children into the boat. First Officer Murdoch came and told Officer Pitman to get into the boat too and take charge of its evacuation, before asking him to try to stay around the right rear gangway door in case his boat was needed. First Officer Murdoch wished him well as he departed.

Third Officer Pitman remembered, 'There was not the slightest suspicion of panic', as he, along with Quartermaster Olliver, gave the order to lower lifeboat 5. Just before the procedure started, Bruce Ismay was becoming over-anxious, and on grabbing the falls he shouted to Fifth Officer Lowe: 'Lower away! Lower away!' Lowe did not know who he was and shouted back in a harsh voice, apparently also using expletives, 'If you get the hell out of the way, we'll be able to do something! You want me to lower faster? You'll have me drown the lot of them!'

Eleanor Cassebeer stated that just after the collision 'things felt weird', and she became suspicious when she noticed that the lid of her trunk in cabin D31 was not level, and sensed that *Titanic* was leaning forward a bit. She met up with another New Yorker named Harry Anderson, who escorted her to lifeboat 5.

In cabin C148 was 26-year-old Karl Behr, who had been a member of the American Davis Cup lawn tennis team of 1907, the year he had also reached the men's doubles final at Wimbledon. In his circle of friends on ship were Richard and Sarah 'Sallie' Beckwith in cabin D35, and Mrs Beckwith's 19-year-old daughter from a previous marriage, Helen Newsom, who was in cabin D47 – all of New York – along with first-class passengers Edwin and Susan Kimball, who were in cabin D19.

Miss Newsom was a friend of Mr Behr's sister, and they had become romantically involved. Possibly because of the seven-year age gap, Mrs Beckwith did not approve of the relationship, so she had arranged for the family to go on a 'Grand Tour' of Europe to keep them apart for a while. The Beckwiths embarked at Southampton, and it must have come as a surprise when Mr Behr came on board the ship at Cherbourg. He had called her bluff and invented a business trip to Europe to pursue Helen. Newspapers reported that Karl had proposed to Helen in the lifeboat, and they were married in 1913.

On the night of the collision Mr and Mrs Kimball had actually reported that ice had entered their cabin through the porthole. As they started from their staterooms, orders were already being shouted to put on lifebelts. They did so as quickly as they could and then made their way up to the boat deck. When Mrs Beckwith reached lifeboat 5, she asked Bruce Ismay if men could get in too. 'Certainly, madam,' Mr Ismay replied. Mr Ismay then called out, 'Are there any more to get into this boat?' but none appeared, so Mr Behr, the Beckwiths and the Kimballs all got in.

Mabel Bennett's sister Emily was married to Alfred Crawford, who was a bedroom steward on the ship, and her nephew Leonard Hoare was a saloon steward who lost his life in the sinking. All three were natives of Southampton. Mabel was wearing only a night dress when she left her cabin, and Alfred warned her that she had better wear something warm for protection against the elements, so she grabbed a fur coat and put it on. Following repeated calls from First Officer Murdoch and Bruce Ismay for women to come forward and take a place in the boat, Mabel appeared and Ismay asked her to get in. Mabel said: 'I am only a stewardess,' and Ismay replied, 'Never mind. You are a woman. Take your place.' She was said to be the last woman to enter lifeboat 5. Mabel wore as she travelled back to England on board *Lapland*, and it was sold at auction in 2017.

Annie Stengel had woken her husband Charles from a dream which was making him stir and moan. They felt a slight jarring of the ship, and they became concerned when they realised that the engines had stopped. They went to investigate and were on A Deck when they saw Captain Smith come up from below looking very grave, which prompted Charles to remark that the situation might be serious. They climbed the stairs to the boat deck and Mrs Stengel got into lifeboat 5, leaving Charles to walk forward towards the emergency lifeboat 1.

Max Frolicher-Stehli was a Swiss businessman who was travelling with his wife, Margaretha and their daughter, Hedwig, who had suffered with seasickness early in the voyage. He had been playing cards in the first-class smoking room with fellow Swiss passengers, Colonel Alfons Simonius of the Swiss Army, and a lawyer named Dr Max Stahelin-Maeglon. On returning to his cabin at about 11:30pm, Max and Margaretha were in bed but not asleep when they felt the collision. Hedwig came into their room quite upset so they went out and looked over the side of the ship, where they saw the iceberg. Eventually they arrived on the boat deck. The two girls were helped into lifeboat 5, and Max was allowed to accompany them when no more females appeared.

Dr Henry Frauenthal, an eminent surgeon, had recently married his new wife, Clara, in Nice, and they were travelling with Henry's brother, Isaac, who had joined them at Cherbourg. Other couple who got into the boat were Norman and Bertha Chambers; Sam and Nella Goldenberg; George and Dorothy Harder; and Elmer and Juliet Cummins.

Canadian-born Spencer Silverthorne was another department store buyer, and an acquaintance of James McGough. He had been reading a cowboy book *The Virginian* in the first-class smoking room when the collision occurred, and an officer advised him to get up to the boat deck. When he got there, lifeboat 7 had been launched, so he got into lifeboat 5.

Doctor Washington Dodge stated: 'The officers in charge of loading the boats were cool and masterful, preventing as far as possible all disorder and enforcing the command to care for women and children first.' Doctor Dodge was travelling from San Francisco with his wife, Ruth, and their son Washington Junior. They had been in France to try to find a treatment for Washington's skin disease, and had boarded at Southampton, occupying first-class cabin A34. After he had helped his wife and son into lifeboat 5, Doctor Dodge watched it progress in dangerous stops and starts as it lowered down towards the water. As he looked over the side and saw the 90-feet drop, he became 'overwhelmed with doubts' that he may have put them in more danger than they would have been if they had stayed on the ship. The doctor escaped in lifeboat 13. However, in 1919 he suffered a nervous breakdown and committed suicide.

Third Officer Pitman kept lifeboat 5 near the gangway as he had been asked, but when it did not open, they rowed away for about a hundred yards to avoid being caught in any suction that might be created as the ship went down. Lifeboat 7 was still close by with George Alfred Hogg and fellow lookout Archie Jewell in charge, and as the two boats got close together, they decided to transfer four passengers from number 5 to number 7 lifeboat.

Third Officer Pitman saw lifeboat 3 being lowered and watched in horror as the front of the massive ship got lower and lower in the water and the different rows of lights disappeared under the surface. However, he said that he did not give up hope until he saw the last line of lights on the forecastle head disappear. When asked if he knew the time when *Titanic* disappeared from the surface, he replied: 'Two-twenty, exactly, ship's time. I took my watch out at the time she disappeared, and I said, "It is 2:20," and the passengers around me heard it.'

It must have been heartbreaking to hear the cries coming from the drowning people, and although the officer suggested that they go back, several passengers were against it, and they persuaded him not to. One woman practically begged him not to go back: 'Why should we lose our lives in a useless attempt to save others from the ship?' Third Officer Pitman eventually gave in to the pleas, but it was a decision he was to regret for the rest of his life.

He remembered that at about this time, he saw what he thought was a white light from the stern of a sailing ship about 5 miles away. When they got about 200 yards north of the starboard side of where *Titanic* sank, they stopped rowing and rested on their oars.

They endured freezing weather for hours, and Ruth Dodge was particularly affected by it. Quartermaster Olliver helped her as best he could by offering her his socks, stating, 'I assured you, ma'am, they are perfectly clean. I just put them on this morning.'

LIFEBOAT 3

Lifeboat 3 became the third vessel launched from the starboard forward section of the ship. First Officer Murdoch and Fifth Officer Lowe supervised the action. This boat had similar problems to that which lifeboat 7 had suffered, descending in fits and starts, as the lowering ropes became stuck in the pulleys, but it eventually reached the water, where Able Seaman George Moore took control of the tiller.

Quartermaster George Rowe had been on duty on the poop deck, where he saw a mass of ice pass by very close to the starboard side of the ship. He noticed a lifeboat had been launched in that vicinity. He was asked to collect some distress rockets and take them up to the Bridge. On arrival, he was met by Fourth Officer Boxhall, and as the time was approaching 1am, they both began the task of firing off the flares.

Able Seaman Moore had been off watch and in bed when the collision occurred, which he described as sounding like 'a cable running out, like a ship dropping anchor.' When he got to the boat deck, he assisted in launching lifeboats 7 and 5, and after he helped swing out lifeboat 3, he was ordered into the craft to take charge. Ten other crewmen got on board. Also in the boat was Fireman John Haggan, who had served with the Royal Horse Artillery during the Boer War, and had been present as an escort at the funeral of Queen Victoria. Another member of the crew on board was Wilfred Seward, who worked as the chief pantry steward in second class. He was called to testify at the British Board of Control inquiry.

An American publisher of *Harper's Weekly* named Henry Harper, who had only narrowly escaped being a victim of a sinking in 1883, was travelling with his wife, Myra. They had boarded at Cherbourg on their way back from a five-month tour of North Africa. They had with them a newly employed interpreter named Hammad Hassab, who Mr Harper had taken on in Cairo because he had been amused when Hassab said he, 'wanted to see the country all the crazy Americans come from.' Also with them was Mrs Harper's Pekingese dog named

Sun yat-sen. Unfortunately, Henry was ill with tonsillitis and spent most of the voyage in his D33 cabin, presumably on the starboard side of the ship.

Henry and Myra were asleep in their room when Henry was woken up by what he described as a grinding noise, and he looked out of the porthole to see, 'an iceberg only a few feet away, racing aft at a high speed and crumbling as it went.' They both put on heavy coats, leaving Henry's bowler hat on top of the wardrobe, and after being told there were, 'trunks floating around in the cargo hold,' they went up on deck. Deciding that number 3 lifeboat would float the longest of the ones he could see, he observed that there were no other women around and he and his wife, with Hassab and the dog, got into lifeboat 3. He described the crew who were rowing his lifeboat as liking to, 'the young man who hires a boat on Central Park Lake on Sunday and tries to show off.'

Dr Max Stahelin had returned to his stateroom after the card game with his two fellow Swiss compatriots and was just about to undress when he felt a slight thrust and heard a deep rolling sound. He went up to the boat deck, where he met Colonel Simonius and they got into lifeboat 3.

After Harry Anderson had put Eleanor Cassebeer in lifeboat 5, he took a place in lifeboat 3, followed at some point by Thomas Cardeza, who was a wealthy American banker of French heritage. After some big game hunting on safari in Africa, he had boarded at Cherbourg with his mother Charlotte, a wealthy widow; his French servant, Louis Lesueur, who was in first-class cabin B101; and his mother's Scottish maid, Annie Moor Ward. They had occupied some of the most luxurious suites on the ship in cabins B51, B53 and B55, which cost over £500.

On the night of the sinking Annie did not dress fully. She had thrown a fur coat over her nightdress and grabbed a few of Mrs Cardeza's possessions such as some jewellery and silver condiments from a dressing table, putting them in her pockets. Later she offered them back to Mrs Cardeza, but she was allowed to keep them. They had left behind fourteen trunks, four suitcases and three crates of baggage. Charlotte Cardeza put in a claim to recover £26,000 for the loss of her wardrobe and other effects. Her inventory includes a Burma ruby ring valued at £3,000, a pink diamond valued at £4,000, £100-worth of hatpins, and a white petticoat estimated at £20.

The Speddens were returning to New York from a holiday on the French Riviera and boarded at Cherbourg. Their party included Frederic Spedden, his wife Margaret, who was usually known as Daisy;

their son Robert; Daisy's Irish maid, Helen Wilson; and Robert's nanny, Elizabeth Burns, who Robert referred to as 'Muddie Boons'. After the collision they felt the ship listing, so Daisy woke the others and told Robert they were taking 'a trip to the stars'. The whole party got into lifeboat 3.

Also in lifeboat 3 was first-class passenger Adolf Saalfeld. He was a self-made businessman who had brought on board with him a black leather satchel containing sixty-five small glass vials of various perfume fragrances, which he intended to take to America to take advantage of the expanding market there. They seem to be the fragrances that were popular in the Edwardian period such as Lily of the Valley, Blushing Rose and Orange Blossom. He had been in the first-class smoking, room from where he had seen the iceberg. He returned to his cabin and when he sensed there was a problem, he went up on deck seeking information. When he got there, he recorded: 'I saw a few men and women go into a lifeboat and I followed.' He had that day's menu from the Café Parisien in his pocket, but to his dismay he had forgotten to collect his black satchel when he left his cabin. Some sources say that he entered a lifeboat that was launched later, but his account suggests that he reached the boat deck soon after the collision, and it is likely that he would have remembered to retrieve his satchel if he had allowed himself more time on the ship.

Edith Graham was a wealthy American who had been on a visit in Europe and boarded *Titanic* at Southampton, with her teenage daughter Margaret and her governess Elizabeth Shutes. Edith was in cabin C91, while Elizabeth and Margaret were in C125. After the collision had occurred, they had been told that nothing was wrong, but Margaret had been eating a chicken sandwich when it happened and became so uneasy that she could not keep her hands steady and the chicken pieces kept falling from the bread.

When they got to the boat deck they were helped to lifeboat 3 by two Americans named Washington Roebling and Howard Case. Margaret remembered that the last she saw of Mr Case was him leaning over the rail calmly smoking a cigarette. At first, they preferred to stay close to the ship, hoping that the problem could be fixed and they could go back on board. Miss Shutes remembered sitting next to Clara Hays and her daughter Orian, and they all huddled together to keep warm.

Charles Melville Hays was the president of the Grand Trunk Transcontinental Railway Company. He had been in London on business and wanted to get back to Canada for the gala opening of his new hotel, and he and his wife Clara had received news that their daughter Louise was having difficulty with her pregnancy. They occupied cabin B69, and their 27-year-old daughter Orian and her husband Thornton Davidson were with them in cabin B71. Thornton was the son of a Canadian lawyer and judge, and was an accomplished sportsman at sailing, hockey, lawn tennis and riding. Also in the party were their Canadian maid Mary Perreault, and Mr Hays' Canadian secretary Vivian Payne, in first-class cabin B24. They were later moved to B73 so Mr Hays could have closer access to his secretary. While she was in London Mary had accepted a proposal of marriage, and Mr Payne was described as a very popular man, who was astonished at how green the countryside was in England in March.

When disaster struck, the whole party made their way up to the boat deck. Mr Hays made sure his wife and daughter, and Mary, had got into lifeboat 3, and then moved away, making no attempt to enter any of the lifeboats. He, Mr Davidson and Mr Payne all lost their lives. There is a memorial to Thornton Davidson at Mount Royal Cemetery in Montreal, Canada.

It seems that some of the bored passengers in lifeboat 3 argued with each other as the freezing night went on, and they were rescued by *Carpathia* at about 7:30am.

On 8 December 2024, the *Antiques Roadshow* television programme visited Beaumaris Castle on Anglesey, where one of the items presented was a rowlock mounted on a wooden block and bearing the inscription 'Titanic lifeboat number 3', which had been found in a garage in Llandudno. The expert could not confirm that the artefact was from a *Titanic* lifeboat and did not value it. However, as a point of interest, Fifth Officer Lowe helped to launch lifeboat 3, and later lived and died in north Wales and is buried at Colwyn Bay, close to Llandudno.

EMERGENCY LIFEBOAT 1

Lifeboats on the portside of the ship had started to be launched at about 12:30am, and this craft may not have been the next lifeboat in sequence, but emergency lifeboat 1 was the front vessel of the four on the starboard side, and was the fourth and last to be launched by First Officer Murdoch and Fifth Officer Lowe, at about 1:05am, and Lookout George Symons was placed in charge. It had a capacity for forty people but only twelve eventually got in, the fewest to escape in any single lifeboat that night. It prompted a greaser who was standing at a lower deck named Wally Hurst to remark, 'If they are sending the boats away, they might as well put some people in them.'

Despite the 'women and children first' drill, Fifth Officer Lowe allowed seven male members of the crew and only five passengers to get into the lifeboat, of which only two were women – Lady Duff-Gordon and her secretary.

When the lifeboat had descended to about B Deck it encountered a spar, an obstacle such as a piece of rigging sticking out like a pole from the side of the ship, which became trapped under the gunwale (the piece of metal fitted around the top of the boat to strengthen it) and the procedure was stopped abruptly. The crew had to cut at the obstacle with wire cutters to free the craft, and it did not reach the water until about 1:15am. First Officer Murdoch and Fifth Officer Lowe shouted down to them a last instruction that they should row away from the ship as fast as they could, and having seven crew members in the boat it was not long before they had rowed some distance and Lady Duff-Gordon's secretary, Laura Francanelli said they 'were a long way off' when they saw *Titanic* go right up at the back and plunge down. 'There was an awful rumbling when she went. Then came the screams and cries. I do not know how long they lasted.'

George Symons and fellow West Countryman Archie Jewell were lookouts who usually worked together, and they had been relieved of their duties when the collision occurred. The rest of the crewmen were Leading Fireman Charles Hendrickson, who had previously been tasked to help to try to put out the fire in the bunkers, and Fireman John Collins, a former Royal Marine, who may have served in the Anglo-Boer War of 1899–1902. The other two firemen were George Taylor, who signed on using his brother's name of James, and William Pusey, usually known as Robert, who stated at the United States Inquiry that Lady Gordon said to Miss Franks [Francatelli] as they looked back at the ship, 'There is your beautiful nightdress gone.' To which Pusey replied, 'Never mind about your nightdress, madam, as long as you have got your life.' The numbers in emergency lifeboat 1 were made up by Trimmer Frederick Sheath and Able Seaman Albert Horswill.

Albert Horswill was the son of a Devon policeman, and a former member of the Royal Navy. He left the navy and joined the White Star Line. His previous ship had been RMS *Oceanic.* He had worked on getting the lifeboats ready for launch on the portside, where he was ordered to put a lamp and a chronometer into emergency lifeboat 2, and then moved to the starboard side to work on emergency lifeboat 1. He stated that there were incidents when he had had to manhandle reluctant passengers into the lifeboat, but they just scrambled back out again. According to the television programme *QI,* his family did not speak to him after the disaster because they had read that he had accepted a bribe.

Scotsman Sir Cosmo Duff-Gordon and his wife, Lucy, a fashion designer, occupied cabin A16 in the first-class quarters, only one level down from the boat deck. They were travelling with Lucy's secretary, London-born Laura Francatelli, who preferred to be called by her middle name of Mabel and occupied cabin E36, a few levels lower than her employers. Sir Cosmo, a landowner and sportsman, was a member of the International Olympic Committee and had gained an Olympic fencing silver medal at what was known as the Interim Games held in Athens in 1906, to celebrate the tenth anniversary of the first Games held in that city in 1896. He was also a wrestler and took part in the mixed martial arts known as Bartitsu, which was immortalised in the Sherlock Holmes books. A marble bust of him was sold at auction in 2020.

Miss Francatelli had been woken when she realised there was water seeping under her cabin door, and she dashed up to alert her employers. When the trio came out onto the boat deck wearing their life-preservers, Mabel remembered: 'I then noticed that the sea was nearer to us than during the day.' She stated to Sir Cosmo, 'We are sinking.' To which he replied, 'Nonsense, come away.'

Lady Duff-Gordon and Mabel were asked several times to get into one of the three lifeboats that had been loaded and launched on the starboard front of the ship, but they refused because they did not want to leave Sir Cosmo to his fate. Eventually, they were offered seats in emergency lifeboat 1, and Miss Francotelli recalled, 'There were no other women there by that time. The officer saw us and ordered us in, and we said we would go if Sir Cosmo could come also.' The officer decided to allow all three to get in.

As they were about to lower the boat, First Officer Murdoch gave Charles Stengel and another American businessman named Abram Salomon permission to get in. However, as Mr Stengel climbed over a waist-high railing, he stumbled and rolled into the boat and landed in an undignified heap, causing Mr Murdoch to laugh as he remarked, 'That is the funniest sight I have seen tonight.'

A New York wholesale stationer, Abraham Lincoln Salomon, to give him his full name, had been on a business trip to Europe. His 11-year-old daughter Helen had travelled with him but she did not board *Titanic*. The reason why she was not on the ship is not known, but she was later reunited with her parents in New York. Abram retained a *Titanic* luncheon menu for 14 April, and a receipt from the Turkish bath, which he had signed by Mr and Mrs Duff-Gordon.

Some of the crew talked about how they had lost their kits and would have their pay stopped from the time the ship was wrecked. Sir Cosmo or Lady Duff-Gordon overheard them and replied, 'We will give you a little to start a new kit.'

On the following day Sir Cosmo kept to his word and paid the crew members £5 ($20) each – now worth over £300 – which he stated was to help to replace their uniforms and kit, and to help them and their families financially. Some, mainly in the Media, have described the gift as blood money for saving their lives, but why would Sir Cosmo pay them a bribe after he had been saved? The promissory note presented to Able Seaman Albert Horswill still exists.

At one point in time Mr Stengel believed that he saw the lights of a ship about 200 yards off and they rowed towards it. There was not much talking as they all huddled in the bottom of the boat to keep warm.

Despite the problems they had when launching the lifeboat, it was a lighter craft and they had as many as seven crew members to row, so they were rescued by *Carpathia* at about 4:30am, a relatively short time out on the sea, and only emergency lifeboat 2 from the portside had reached the rescue ship previously.

PORTSIDE FRONT

LIFEBOAT 6

Second Officer Lightoller was by lifeboat 6 when he noticed: '...she [the ship] was distinctly down by the head, and I think it was while working at that boat it was noticed she had a pretty heavy list to port.' He continued, 'However, having got Captain Smith's sanction, I indicated to the Bosun's Mate [Albert Haines], and we lowered down the first boat [number 6 at 1:10am] down to the boat deck, and, just at this time, thank heaven, the frightful din of the escaping steam suddenly stopped, and there was a death-like silence.'

The captain then gave the order to load women and children into lifeboat 6 and Second Officer Lightoller began the task by himself. He: 'stood with one foot on the seat just inside the gunwale of the boat, and the other foot on the ship's deck, and the women merely held out their wrist, their hand, and I took them by the wrist and hooked their arm underneath my arm.'

Quartermaster Hichens had come on duty in the wheelhouse at 8pm that night, and at 10pm he took the helm off Quartermaster Olliver in control of the ship. At 11:40pm he heard three bells struck from the lookout post, and then the commander shouted, 'Hard-a-starboard.' However, there was not enough time for the manoeuvre and the ship collided with the iceberg.

Quartermaster Hichens was ordered by Second Officer Lightoller to get in lifeboat 6 and take charge. As the boat was being lowered, Hichens shouted back up to the boat deck that the boat was badly manned. Second Officer Lightoller called for assistance from anyone who had experience of the sea, and a Canadian businessman in the form of Major Arthur Peuchen stepped forward and offered his services, stating his experience as a yachtsman with the Royal Canadian Yacht Club. The major was a chemical manufacturer and formerly an officer of the Queen's Own Rifles of Canada, who had acted as marshalling officer at the coronation of King George V and Queen Mary on 22 June 1911.

Captain Smith suggested that the major should go down to the promenade deck so he could break a window and access the boat from there, but Second Officer Lightoller was of the opinion that if he was as good a sailor as he claimed, he should be capable of sliding down the ropes to get into the boat. Major Peuchen then grabbed a rope and climbed down hand-over-hand to the boat.

Ruth Bowker and Mabel Martin were the only two females who worked in the à la carte restaurant, being employed as cashiers. Ruth was a twin, and the daughter of a former Derbyshire doctor who had only recently passed away, and Mabel was a London girl on her first ever sea voyage. They were still working in their office when the collision occurred, which Ruth described as 'a slight shock, and a curious grating noise.' When she got on deck, she became aware that the engines had stopped and there was a deafening noise as they were blowing off steam. Ruth was on her way back to her cabin when she met Thomas Andrews, who told her the ship was going down. Alarmed at his remark, she went back on deck and was standing at the portside of the front of the ship, where she and Mabel were told by Captain Smith to get into lifeboat 6. Showing a reluctance to do so, Ruth said that she was 'dragged in' by one of the sailors. The boat was lowered 'with some difficulty.' When the two men and a boy who were rowing became exhausted, Ruth and Mabel took over the oars. As they rowed away from the doomed ship, Ruth watched her lights blazing and described it as 'a spectacle of fairy-like beauty.'

Described as a 'Strikingly beautiful woman', Helen Candee, a feminist and writer from New York, had been touring Europe doing research for a book she was working on when she received a telegram from her daughter advising her that her son had been injured in an accident, and she immediately booked a ticket on *Titanic* for the journey home. Edward Kent was a regular passenger on transatlantic ships, and he had just spent two months in Europe when he boarded as a first-class passenger on *Titanic.*

The two members of 'Our Coterie' were rushing up to the boat deck when they met each other. Mrs Candee noticed Mr Kent had pockets, so she handed him a small flask of brandy and asked him to accept an ivory and gold antique cameo brooch of her mother for safe-keeping. They were obviously not aware of the 'women and children first' rule, because Mrs Candee thought Mr Kent had a better chance of surviving than her. When they arrived on the boat deck, Mr Kent escorted Mrs Candee into lifeboat 6 and stepped back, but as Helen was boarding the craft she slipped and injured herself. Edward Kent lost his life in the sinking, and when his body was retrieved from the Atlantic by the cable ship *Mackay-Bennett*, the jewel was recovered and returned to Mrs Candee.

Mother and daughter Elsie and Edith Bowerman were active suffragettes and friends of Emmeline Pankhurst. As recently as Saturday, 6 April 1912, Elsie had attended an open-air meeting of suffragettes in Hastings, to support the cause. They were on their way to visit relations in Ohio and then planned to travel across the United States and Canada. They occupied cabin D33, and Elsie wrote, 'The silence when the engines stopped was followed by a steward knocking on the door and telling us to go up on deck. This we did and were lowered into lifeboats, when we were told to get away from the liner as soon as we could because of suction. This we did, and to pull an oar in the midst of the Atlantic in April with icebergs floating about is a strange experience.'

New Yorkers Edgar and Leila Meyer had received news that Leila's father had passed away, and they had hastily arranged their passage on *Titanic*. They had dined in the Café Parisien and were in their cabin when the collision occurred. When they arrived at lifeboat 6, Leila pleaded with Edgar to either get into the craft with her, or to allow her to remain on deck so that they might live or die together. Edgar refused and forcibly made her get into the lifeboat, reminding her of their 9-year-old child at home.

Lucian and Mary Eloise Smith were on an extended honeymoon and had boarded *Olympic*, under the command of Captain Smith, for a trip around the world. Lucian came from a family with large coal interests, and Eloise was a member of a family involved in politics. However, they became home sick for the mountains of West Virginia, and on cutting their journey short, they boarded *Titanic* at Cherbourg as first-class passengers in cabin C31.

On the night of the collision Lucian came away from his card game with Pierre Marechal, Paul Chevre and Alfred Omont, and went to the cabin and woke Eloise, telling her, 'We are in the north Atlantic and have struck an iceberg. It does not amount to anything but will probably delay us a day getting into New York. However, as a matter of form, the captain has ordered all ladies on deck.' When they got to the boat deck, after Captain Smith had ignored Eloise's request that Lucian should join her in a lifeboat, Lucian helped Eloise into lifeboat 6, assuring her that he would be given a place in another lifeboat once all the women and children had been evacuated, and in kissing her goodbye, he advised her to keep her hands in her pockets. Lucian's three French card companions were all rescued earlier in lifeboat 7, but Lucian lost his life in the sinking, not knowing that his new wife was in the early stages of pregnancy.

While on board *Carpathia*, Eloise met Robert Williams Daniel, a bank executive, who had been on a business trip to London and had boarded at Southampton for his fifth transatlantic voyage back to Philadelphia. His first-class stateroom was on A Deck near the front of the ship. He had with him an expensive champion French bulldog named Gamin de Pycombe (The Pycombe Kid – Pycombe being a village near Brighton) which he had bought in England. When the ship stopped at Cherbourg, he sent a brief telegram to his mother in Richmond to let her know that he was 'on board *Titanic*.' His dog did not survive, and Eloise gave birth to Lucian junior later in the year. She married Robert, but they later divorced and she married three more times after him.

Margaret 'Molly' Brown was an American human-rights activist and philanthropist, known for her flashy hats and charming personality. She had spent some time in Egypt and then Paris as part of the Jacob Astor party, until she had received word from Denver that her eldest grandchild, Lawrence, was ill. She booked passage home on the first available ship going to New York, and boarded *Titanic* at Cherbourg.

Molly was a multi-linguist and using that skill, she helped to get other passengers into lifeboats, before finally getting into lifeboat 6. She and some of the other women in the boat helped to row and keep up the spirits of the other passengers to dispel the gloom that was apparently being voiced by Quartermaster Hichens. On *Carpathia* she assisted other survivors, established the Survivor's Committee, was elected chairperson, and raised almost $10,000 for destitute survivors. She remained on the rescue ship until all the survivors had been collected by friends and family or had medical and emergency assistance. She presented a solver loving cup to the captain of the *Carpathia* on recognition of his rescue of *Titanic* survivors.

Martin and Elizabeth Rothschild were New Yorkers who had boarded at Cherbourg as first-class passengers; Mr Rothschild was a clothing manufacturer, who perished in the sinking. They had with them a Pomeranian dog which they kept in their cabin, and which Elizabeth managed to keep undetected on board lifeboat 6, until they reached the rescue ship at about 6am. The crew of *Carpathia* refused to allow the dog on board, but Mrs Rothschild insisted that she would not climb the ladder without it. It was one of only three dogs that survived the disaster.

Several passengers made not too complimentary remarks about Quartermaster Hichens' behaviour in the lifeboat, including Leila Meyer, who accused him of being drunk. In his defence he stated:

I would like to make a little statement as regarding Mrs Meyer's statement in the newspapers about my drinking the whisky, sir, and about the blankets. I was very cold, sir, and I was standing up in the boat. I had no hat on. A lady had a flask of whisky or brandy, or something of that description, given her by some gentleman on the ship before she left, and she pulled it out and gave me about a tablespoonful and I drank it. Another lady, who was lying in the bottom of the boat, in a rather weak condition gave me a half wet and half dry blanket to try keeping myself a little warm, as I was half frozen. I think it was very unkind of her, sir, to make any statement criticizing me. When we got to the ship I handled everyone as carefully as I could, and I was the last one to leave the boat, and I do not think I deserve anything like that to be put in the papers. That is what upset me and got on my nerves.

LIFEBOAT 8

At 1am lifeboat 8 was the second to be launched from the portside forward, by First Officer Wilde and Second Officer Lightoller, with Captain Smith also lending a hand. Able Seaman Thomas Jones, of Anglesey, was placed in charge, and the craft was filled to less than half of its capacity.

The 67-year-old American millionaire and co-owner of the famous Macey's department store, Isidor Straus, and Ida, his wife of forty years, had been in Europe since January 1912. They were looking for a new French maid but without success. They did manage to hire a British maid, but she left them just before they embarked at Cherbourg and a London girl named Ellen Bird was given the job. Also in the party was Isidor's English manservant, John Farthing.

Mr Straus was offered a place in lifeboat 8 but he refused saying, 'I do not wish any distinction in my favour which is not granted to others.' When Ida was asked to join a group of people who were waiting to get into the boat, she said, 'I will not be separated from my husband. As we have lived, so we will die – together.' Then she gave her fur coat to Ellen, and insisted that she should get in. As the lifeboats were being rowed away from the stricken vessel, the couple were seen to be consoling each other and awaiting their inevitable fate. John Farthing was also a victim.

Lizzie Bonnell, known as Lily, was travelling in first class with her niece, Caroline Bonnell, her maternal brother-in-law Colonel George Wick, his wife Mary, known as Molly, and their daughter Nathalie. Caroline was the daughter of Lizzie's oldest brother, John Meek, who had become a successful iron and steel merchant in Chicago, until his death in 1884. They had been travelling in Europe in an effort to help with George's bad health, and while in Paris they had met and become friends with Washington Roebling and Stephen Blackwell, who were also travelling on *Titanic.* They had all agreed to meet Lily at Southampton, and Lily planned to go back to Ohio for a six-month visit. Lily occupied cabin C103, while cousins Caroline and Natalie were in cabin C7.

Caroline Bonnell remembered:

'Nathalie Wick and I were lying in our berths half asleep when the blow came. It was terrible. For a second the whole boat just stood stock still in its swift tracks, and then it gave a great shiver all through. When we got out onto the deck everything was as calm as an August afternoon. The sea was as smooth as glass. There wasn't a berg or an ice floe in sight, and the sky was just thick with stars. I never saw so many stars in my life as there were that night. The water glittered blue with their glow. We had just decided to go back to bed when an officer came up to us and to another group of people who had gotten up to find out what was the matter.

'Go below, and put on your lifebelts,' he said, 'you may need them later.'

We went down at once and told my aunt and uncle, Mr and Mrs George Wick, what we had been told. Uncle George just laughed at us.

'Why, that's nonsense girls,' he said. 'This boat is all right. She's going along nicely. She just got a glancing blow, I guess.'

That's the way everyone seemed to thing, and we went into our stateroom, but in a minute or so an officer knocked at the door and told us to go up on the A Deck. He said that there was really no danger and it was just a precautionary measure.

When we got on the deck my uncle and aunt were there, and I went down again to another part of the steamer and got my Aunt Elizabeth. When I got back with her, there were crowds of people standing all around. Nobody seemed very excited; everyone was talking, and it seemed to be the general idea that we would soon be ordered back to bed. Just then an officer came up to us and said we should go up to the next deck – the boat deck! By that time everyone was up, Mrs John Jacob Astor was there, sitting in a steamer chair. Her husband, Colonel Astor, was beside her, and her maid was helping her to finish her dressing. There was no confusion here even yet, though we noticed that the boat was beginning to list to starboard.

The Bonnell ladies were placed in lifeboat 8, and Caroline continued:

In the lifeboats it was terrible. Some of the women had scarcely any clothes on at all, and they suffered greatly with the cold. One woman had light satin slippers and an evening dress on. I don't know whether she had that attire on when we struck, or whether, in her excitement, she put it on by mistake.

> We were provided with the most miserable little oil lamps I have ever seen. I guess it didn't have any kerosene in it, for it kept going out as fast as we could light it with the matches which the steward happened to bring along. We couldn't have seen at all nor signalled had it not been for the fact that one woman had a cane that had a little electric light in the end of it. As far as I know there was no food or water in the craft, but I will not complain of that for we were the luckiest, I guess, of all the survivors. The other boats all leaked, and the women told us afterwards that the water was up to their knees. And that water was below freezing point, 31 degrees to be even.

Two of the oars were lost overboard, probably due to the effect of the cold on the rowers' hands. Caroline stated that there was a small lamp in the boat which was difficult to keep alight.

Emma Bucknell and her maid Albina Bassani were in cabin D15. Emma related that ice had fallen through a broken porthole, so she and Albina dressed warmly. Back in the corridor she saw two young women talking, one of whom would not believe that the ship had hit an iceberg, so Emma went to the end of the corridor, scooped up some ice and went back and showed it to her. They went up to A Deck, where an officer told them to go back to their cabins and put on their lifebelts. When they got back up to A Deck an officer told them that a lifeboat was waiting for them on the boat deck. As they climbed the stairs, Mrs Bucknell became overcome with nerves and had to be brought a glass of water. When she felt better, they got into lifeboat 8. They helped to row the craft until their hands became blistered.

Ella White was a wealthy New York widow known for her eccentric lifestyle, who was travelling with her friend Grice Young. They had boarded at Cherbourg after spending the winter in Rome, along with Mrs White's maid Nellie Bassette, who was of French descent, and her Italian man servant named Sante Righini, who was living in New York at that time. While in Europe they had purchased some expensive live chickens which they had stored in the cargo hold. Mrs White was sporting an injured foot and spent most of the voyage in bed. When she did get about, she had to use a cane, which had a light at the end of it.

All the females in the party boarded lifeboat 8, but when Mr Righini tried to get in the boat with them, someone stopped him by smashing an oar on his fingers and forced him to back off. He lost his life in the sinking. When they were in the lifeboat Mrs White waved her cane about to provide some light, and the passengers burned what they could find to try to make themselves visible to any rescue ship's crew. Mrs White was very critical of the conduct of the crewmen in the lifeboat, who she said had no idea of what to do with the oars. Only Able Seaman Jones at the tiller seemed to know what he was doing.

Margaret Swift and Doctor Alice Leader shared cabin D17 and had made friends with Fred and Marion Kenyon during the trip. Mrs Swift and Dr Leader were both widows, and Dr Leader was a New York physician. While in their cabin they were visited by a man holding ice in his hands, and as they made their way to the boat deck, they saw that there was ice all over the corridors and under the portholes. They managed to get to lifeboat 8, where all three women boarded. Marion asked Fred to follow them, but he refused to do so, stating that he would wait until all the women and children were accounted for. They never saw him again.

Dr Leader stated: 'The Countess [Rothes] is an expert oarswoman, and thoroughly at home on the water. She practically took command of the boat when it was found that the seamen who had been placed at the oars could not row skilfully. Several of the women took their place, with the countess at the oars and rowed in turns, while the weak and unskilled stewards sat quietly in one end of the boat.'

Noelle Leslie, the wife of the nineteenth Earl of Rothes, embarked with her parents at Southampton, along with her cousin Gladys Cherry, and her maid Roberta Maioni. Her parents disembarked at Cherbourg. Miss Cherry had become well-known for her charity work in the UK. She and the countess manned the tiller alternately, each steering for over an hour at a time. During their breaks they spent time trying to comfort Maria Penasco, whose husband Victor was lost in the sinking. 'Poor woman!' the countess related, 'Her sobs tore our hearts, and her moans were unspeakable in their sadness.'

Gladys Cherry wrote a letter to Able Seaman Jones in which she stated:

> ...how splendidly you took charge of the boat on that fateful night – and I think you were wonderful. The dreadful regret I shall always have, and I know you share with me, is that we ought to have gone back to see whom we could pick up, but if you remember, there was only an American lady, my cousin, self and you who wanted to return. I could not hear the discussion very clearly, as I was at the tiller, but everyone forward and the three men refused; but I shall always remember your words: 'Ladies, if any of us are saved, remember, I wanted to go back. I would rather drown with them than leave them.' You did all you could, and being my own countryman, I wanted to tell you this.

As a parting gift when they reached New York, the Countess presented Able Seaman Jones with a silver pocket watch as a thank you for saving her life, and in return he gave her a plaque displaying the number '8' taken from the lifeboat in which they had met. They maintained correspondence for the rest of their lives, and the countess wrote to the Jones family every Christmas, always including a pound note. The watch eventually returned to the countess's family.

EMERGENCY LIFEBOAT 2

Emergency lifeboat 2 was launched by Chief Officer Wilde and Fourth Officer Boxhall at about 1:40am or just after, from the portside forward; with the operation being overseen by Captain Smith. Other crew members in the boat were Able Seaman Frank Osman; First Class Saloon Steward James Johnstone, a Scotsman who also worked as a night watchman from 11pm, and Assistant Vegetable Cook John Ellis.

Frank Osman had lost his second child as an infant in the previous year. He had been waiting for the bell to ring to signal the start of his shift, but instead of the usual chime he heard three bells ring, which usually meant there was a ship ahead of them; however, soon afterwards he felt the impact of the collision. He went out into the forward well deck and saw large amounts of ice, some of which he collected and took back to his quarters on D Deck. He received orders to go up to the boat deck, and he and some of his mates responded to the order. When they got there, he assisted in the lowering of a few lifeboats on the starboard side, before helping to launch emergency lifeboat 2 and then getting on board to help with the rowing.

Fourth Officer Boxhall had been somewhere in the vicinity of the officers' quarters when he heard the lookout bell, and as he made his way to the Bridge, he recalled that he heard Officer Murdoch give the order 'Hard-a-starboard!' just before the ship's impact with the iceberg. In steamships this meant to turn the wheel to the right to send the vessel in that direction, like a car, although in sailing ships the wheel was turned to the left to make the rudder guide the ship to the right. Then immediately after the collision, the order was given, 'Full speed, astern!' First Officer Murdoch then pulled the lever to close the water-tight doors.

Fourth Officer Boxhall then went along the length of the starboard side of one of the lower decks to try to provide a damage assessment, but he could not see any. However, on C Deck he came upon a man who was carrying a lump of ice, and he took it from him. He returned to the Bridge and reported that he had not seen any actual damage to the ship. His next mission was to find a carpenter, who told him that the ship was taking on water fast, and a man from the mail room also stated that there was water in the ship's hold. On reaching the mail room, Fourth Officer Boxhall was alarmed to discover that the water: 'was rising rapidly up the ladder and I could hear it rushing in.' He saw mailbags floating around in the water. He reported what he had seen to the men on the Bridge, and then he went to the officers' quarters to warn the men who were off-duty. Then he heard the disturbing order that they should get the lifeboats ready, so he went up and down the boat deck on both sides of the ship to help with the unlacing and initial preparation of the lifeboats.

Firearms were stored on ships as a precaution against piracy or mutinies, and it is believed there were four Webley .455 calibre pistols on *Titanic.* Looking towards the rear of the ship, the officers noticed that some of the passengers and crew who were assembling there realised they were in great danger and were starting to panic.

Second Officer Lightoller stated:

> It was about this time that the chief officer [Wilde] came over from the starboard side and asked if I knew where the firearms were... I told the chief officer, 'Yes, I know where they are. Come along and I'll get them for you,' and into the first officer's cabin we went – the chief, Murdoch, the captain and myself – where I hauled them out, still in all their pristine newness and grease. I was going out when the chief shoved one of the revolvers into my hand, with a handful of ammunition, and said, 'Here you are, you may need it.'

There is no evidence that the captain had a revolver, so based on evidence, the pistols were taken by Chief Officer Wilde, First Officer Murdoch, Second Officer Lightoller and Purser McElroy.

On their return, and before they had chance to load the weapons, Chief Officer Wilde and Second Officer Lightoller saw a group of men trying to take over the emergency lifeboat, and several of them had already got into the boat and sat down. Knowing that they had not yet loaded their weapons, they pointed their empty guns at them and Chief Officer Wilde shouted, 'Get out of there, you damned cowards! I'd like to see every one of you overboard!' The bluff worked and they all clambered back onto the deck.

Most of the occupants in emergency lifeboat 2 were women and children, and the only man seems to have been a third-class Austrian passenger named Anton Kink-Heilmann, who was allowed to join his German wife Luise and their daughter of the same name in the boat after they had cried out to him. They had boarded with a party of fellow Austrians and Anton occupied cabin E58 at the back of the ship, with his brother Vincenz, Albert Wirz, Joseph Arnold, Leo Zimmermann and probably Wenzel Linhart.

Mrs Elisabeth Robert, with her daughter Georgette Madill, her niece Elisabeth Allen, and her German-born personal maid Emilie Kreuchen, were actually summoned to get into the collapsible 2 by a whistle. Mrs Robert had been twice widowed, and Georgette was the daughter of her first husband, an eminent judge. She was one of the wealthiest women in St Louis, living in 'The handsomest house in the city.' She was also known for her keen intellect and philanthropy work. Her second husband, a prominent St Louis attorney, had died the previous year and they had all spent a vacation in Europe. Mrs Robert stayed in cabin B3, while Georgette and her cousin were in B5.

Miss Kreuchen had stepped out of her cabin, which was forward on E Deck, into a passageway filled with water. After being told by a purser that parts of the ship were being blocked off to slow the flow of the water, she went to the cabin of Georgette and Elisabeth and warned them that the baggage room was full of water. Miss Allen reminded her that the watertight doors would be shut and that it would be alright. However, when Miss Kreuchen got back to her cabin, it was flooded. All three were eventually rescued in emergency lifeboat 2.

Walter Douglas was described as 'A captain if industry.' His Scottish father had brought together several oatmeal companies to form the Quaker Oats Company, famous for its porridge breakfast cereal, which Walter took over as an executive. His wife Mahala was reported as not being too confident concerning her looks, stating that she once heard a man say, 'too bad about Pet Dutton's nose, I do hope she'll grow into it.' However, after being something of a mischievous girl, she grew to be a confident woman, known for her elegant style and an alluring personality which was attractive to men, and after becoming a widow, she became Walter's second wife.

Walter had retired on the first day of 1912, and they had planned the building of a new mansion, which Mahala referred to as their 'Minnesota Renaissance'. They had been on a three-month tour of Europe looking for furnishings suitable for their new home and had boarded at Cherbourg.

On the night of the collision, they had stayed in their cabin until they saw a lot of people in the corridor wearing lifejackets, so they decided to do the same, Walter having put on his evening dress. They and their maid, Berthe, went up to the boat deck, where Mahala and Berthe got into emergency 2. Walter decided not to get into a lifeboat until all the women and children had been accounted for.

Irish-born Minnie Coutts and her young sons William and Neville were travelling to New York from Kent, to reunite with her husband William, a gold and silver engraver and former Scottish soldier, where they intended to make a new life. The crash had broken her sleep, but she stayed in her bunk for another fifteen minutes. Then she got up and put on some warm clothes, did the same for her sons, including putting lifejackets on them, although she could not find a lifejacket for herself, and went up to the third-class communal area. She could not get through the crowds of people until a sailor came along and said to her, 'Come along, all women and children to the lifeboats,' and he led them to the boat deck. Arriving there she told the crewmen that she had not been able to find a lifejacket. An American man overheard her and stepped forward, took off his lifejacket, and on raising his hat he handed it to her saying, 'Take my life preserver, madam.' Then he patted the two lads on the head, and asked, 'If I go down, please pray for me.'

Fourth Officer Boxhall was busy letting off the distress flares, 'Every time I fired a signal, I had to clear everybody away from the vicinity of the rocket, and then I remember the last one or two distress signals I sent off lifeboat 4 had gone, and they were then working on the collapsible 2 boat which was on the deck.' He remembered that he was sending rockets up right until the time he was sent away in the emergency lifeboat.

Captain Smith told Fourth Officer Boxhall to leave off sending up the flares and to get into the emergency lifeboat to take charge, and after being lowered down to the water, he and the other rowers got the emergency 2 about a hundred yards from the stricken ship and then allowed the craft to drift for a while. Then he heard someone call out from *Titanic* through a megaphone, asking them to bring the lifeboat back towards the starboard stern of the ship. When they got to about 200 feet from the stern, Fourth Officer Boxhall could detect that there was some suction from *Titanic*, so he instructed the rowers to pull hard on the paddles to get the lifeboat away from the ship in a north-easterly direction.

When asked if he heard any cries from the stricken passengers, he replied: 'Yes, I heard cries. I did not know when the lights went out that the ship had sunk. I saw the lights go out, but I did not know whether she had sunk or not, and then I heard the cries. I was showing green lights in the boat then, to try and get the other boats together, trying to keep us all together.'

Despite being one of the last to be launched and having to wait awhile before rowing away from the sinking liner, emergency lifeboat 2 was the first to be rescued, at about 4:10am. Fourth Officer Boxhall spotted *Carpathia* on the horizon just as it started to get light, and guided her to the lifeboats with a green flare, apparently having brought a box of them with him. They had been on the sea for about two and a half hours.

Miss Kreuchen stated:

> While in the lifeboat we were rowed around the stern to the starboard side and away from the ship, as our boat was a small one and Fourth Officer Boxhall feared the suction. We could hear the lapping of the water on the icebergs, but saw none, even when Boxhall lit his green lights, which he did at regular intervals, till we sighted *Carpathia.* Our boat was the first one picked up by the *Carpathia*. I happened to be the first one up the ladder, as the others seemed afraid to start up, and when the officer who received me asked where the *Titanic* was, I told him she had gone down.

LIFEBOAT 4

First Attempt

Chief Officer Henry Wilde and Second Officer Lightoller met as they came out of the officers' quarters. Wilde told him to accompany him to help him to get the covers off the lifeboats, and at about 12:30am Captain Smith and officers Wilde and Lightoller began to uncover lifeboat 4, which was the first on the portside (left) at the front of the ship to get prepared to launch.

Chief Officer Wilde was the tallest officer on board *Titanic.* He joined the White Star Line in 1897 and the Royal Naval Reserve in 1902. Second Officer Charles Lightoller said of him: 'He was a fine fellow and one for whom I had the greatest admiration.' He had served with Captain Smith on *Olympic* and was on board her when she collided with HMS *Hawke.* He had suffered a terrible tragedy when his baby twins had died soon after birth, and his wife died on Christmas Eve 1910.

Second Officer Lightoller stated: 'I commenced stripping off number 4; then two or three turned up. I told them off to number 4 boats and stood off myself and directed the men as they came up on deck, passing around the boat deck, round the various boats, and seeing that the men were evenly distributed around both the port and starboard.'

However, he continued:

> Well, you see, if I may give it to you in the order I was working. I swung out number 4 with the intention of loading all the boats from A deck, the next deck below the boat deck. I lowered number 4 down to A deck, and gave orders for the women and children to go down to A deck to be loaded through the windows. My reason for loading through the windows from A deck was that there was a coaling wire, a very strong wire running along A deck, and I thought that it would be very useful to tie the boat to in case the ship got a slight list or anything, but as I was going down the ladder after giving the order, someone sung out and said the windows were up. I countermanded the order and told

> the people to come back on the boat deck and instructed two or three, I think they were stewards, to find the handles and lower the windows. That left the empty number 4 boat hanging at A deck, so then I went on to number 6.

Second Attempt

Second Officer Lightoller was busy getting the stranded lifeboat 4 to a position where it could be filled with passengers through the windows on A Deck.

Quartermaster Walter Perkis had been on duty for the 6pm to 8pm watch. He was off duty when the collision occurred, and although he had been warned that there was a problem, he remained in his bunk until midnight, when it was time for him to go back on duty. When he got on deck, he assisted in helping to lower lifeboat 4 and then ran to the back of the ship to see what service he could offer there. However, someone shouted out to him (probably Second Officer Lightoller) that he was needed in the number 4 lifeboat, so he ran back, climbed down one of the falls (ropes) and got into the boat, where he assumed command.

Waiting on A Deck was the American millionaire John Jacob Astor; his young wife Madeleine, who was five months pregnant; a valet named Victor Robbins; Madeleine's maid, Rosalie Bidois; and her nurse, Caroline Endres. They also had an Airedale dog with them named Kitty. They had boarded at Cherbourg and occupied one of the parlour suites.

Archibald Gracie stated that when Madeleine was getting through the window, her husband helped her from the other side. When she was in the lifeboat, Mr Astor asked Second Officer Lightoller if he might be allowed to go with her because of her delicate situation.

Second Officer Lightoller replied, 'No, sir, no man is allowed on this boat or any of the boats until the ladies are off.'

Mr Astor then said, 'Well, tell me, what is the number of this boat, so I may find her afterwards?' Second Officer Lightoller informed him that is was lifeboat number 4.

When the three former Lamson sisters' party reached the boat deck, Charlotte and Malvina became separated from Caroline and Edith, and found their way to emergency lifeboat 2, while Caroline and Edith made their way to lifeboat 4. As the craft was about to be lowered, it was decided that it was dangerously overcrowded, and it was ordered that at least one person would have to get back out. Edith got to her feet with the intention of getting off, when Caroline put out her hand to stop her and announced that she would go. However, Edith said determinedly, 'I must be the one to go. You stay, you have children at home and I have nobody.' She climbed out and the lifeboat was lowered. There were three men in the boat and only one of them could row. So Caroline, who was reared on the water, picked up an oar and began to row.

Arthur Ryerson stayed on the deck while the rest of his family got into lifeboat 4. However, when Second Officer Lightoller saw John Borie, he tried to remove him, but Arthur pointed out that he was just a boy and the officer relented and allowed him to stay put. Unknown to the Ryersons, their fourth cousin, William, was working on the ship as a steward. He evacuated in lifeboat 9. Although he was only 13, John Borie was a promising young golfer, who had a successful career in front of him. He is mentioned in *Ripley's Believe it or Not* for the achievement in playing on over 1,000 golf courses during his career.

Marian Thayer and her husband John, who was a director and second vice-president of the Pennsylvania Railroad Company, and a prominent sportsman in his younger days, were rushing back to America after receiving the dreadful news that their son had been killed in a car crash. The party included another son named Jack; Marian's maid, Margaret Fleming; and Grace Bowen, who was a friend of Marian's. They had been travelling in Europe and boarded at Cherbourg. They were getting ready for bed when the collision occurred, and after going up to the boat deck they were led to lifeboat 4, where all the women got in. Marian stated:

> 'We pulled back to where the vessel had sunk, and on our way picked up six men who were swimming – two of whom were drunk and gave us much trouble at the time. The six men picked up were hauled into the boat by the women. Two of these men, a fireman and a steward, died in the boat.
>
> The boat we were in started to take on water; I do not know how. We had to bail. I was standing in ice-cold water up to the top of my boots all the time, and rowing continuously for nearly five hours. We took off about fifteen more people who were standing on a capsized boat. In all, our boat had by that time sixty-five or sixty-six people. There was no room to sit down in our boat, so we all stood, except some sitting along the side.

William and Lucile Carter had attended the coronation of King George V and Queen Mary on 22 June 1911 and were often mentioned on the social pages of newspapers in Britain and America. They had been staying at Melton Mowbray in Leicestershire, to play a few games of his favourite sport and also found time to go hunting with the local foxhounds. When they boarded *Titanic* at Southampton, they had with them their two children, Lucile and William Thornton, along with Lucile's French maid, Auguste Serreplaà; William's Scottish manservant, Alexander Cairns; and the English chauffeur Charles Aldworth. They occupied first-class cabins B96 and B98.

After the dinner party in the à la carte restaurant, the ladies retired and the men played cards in the first-class smoking room, where Mr Carter was when the ship stopped. He went to his cabin and told Lucile to get dressed and head up to the top deck. When they got there, Lucile, Miss Serreplaà and the two children got into lifeboat 4. Lucile kissed her husband goodbye and the lifeboat was lowered. Mr Carter went away and offered to help to load other lifeboats.

Mrs Carter remembered that there were no seamen in the boat, and realising it was a life-or-death situation, she grabbed an oar and started to row, and some of the other women followed suit.

Walter and Virginia Clark had been travelling as part of a belated honeymoon in Europe and had boarded at Cherbourg. Virginia was in her cabin, C89, when she felt the ship hit the iceberg, so she went upstairs to find Walter, who had been playing cards in the smoking lounge. Walter led her to lifeboat 4, where Frank Prentice helped her to get into a lifejacket, before persuading her to leave Walter and get on board. Mrs Clarke remembered that it was supposed to pick up other passengers as it was lowered down to the sea, but logistics prevented it from doing so. The last she saw of Walter was him leaning on the railings waving at her.

At the time of the collision, Assistant Storekeeper Frank Prentice was in his berth on the portside of E Deck, talking to fellow store men Cyril Ricks and Michael Kieran, with whom he was sharing his cabin. Frank noticed that the ship had stopped, so the three men headed up to the promenade deck to investigate and found that the forward well deck was covered in ice. After helping with some of the lifeboats at the rear of the ship, the three men found themselves standing at the portside of the raised section at the back of the ship, known as the poop deck, which was crowded with passengers. They discussed what they should do next and agreed to jump from the ship before she sank. They climbed onto the railings, where Frank noticed a large amount of debris and people floating right beneath them.

Kieran jumped first, followed by Ricks, and then at 2:20am, as the ship began its final plunge to the depths, Prentice jumped and fell about 100 feet into the ice-cold water, narrowly avoiding *Titanic's* massive propellers on the way down, as well as all the debris and people as he hit the water and went under. When he re-surfaced, he was relatively unhurt. He found Ricks, but he had not been so fortunate and had hit some debris as he landed in the water and was seriously hurt. Prentice remained with him until he died from his injuries. He was not able to find Kieran, who lost his life, so he decided to just keep swimming, bumping into many bodies as he did so.

Eventually, he came upon lifeboat 4, which had stayed close to the ship as it sank, and he was pulled on board by some of the occupants. There he met Mrs Clarke again, who wrapped her cloak around him and probably saved him from freezing to death. He tried to drink some whiskey from a bottle, but Quartermaster Perkis grabbed it from him and threw it out of the boat.

They came upon lifeboat 14, with Fifth Officer Lowe in charge. Lifeboats 10, 12 and collapsible D were also in the area. The officer wanted to take his lifeboat back to the disaster area to pick up any survivors, so some passengers were transferred from lifeboat 4 to lifeboat 14. Later, they stayed together with lifeboat 12 and were able to take on board some people who were balancing on the upturned collapsible B. The lifeboat began to take on water and was in danger of being swamped, so they had to row with great effort to get to *Carpathia* when it came in sight.

An 18-carat gold locket engraved with 'VC', which had belonged to Virginia Clarke, was retrieved during a mission to the *Titanic* wreck in 1994.

STARBOARD REAR

LIFEBOAT 9

Lifeboat 9 was the first to be launched from the starboard rear of the vessel, by First Officer Murdoch and Sixth Officer James Moody at about 1:15am. They were assisted by Purser McElroy and Mr Ismay.

James Widgery had completed an inspection of the swimming facility before going to bed. On being wakened by his room-mates, he had arrived at his assigned position at lifeboat 7, but it was already being launched when he got there. Purser Hugh McElroy told Widgery and a saloon steward named William Ward to accompany him to the back of the ship to assist with the loading and launching of lifeboat 9. Widgery was given a box of biscuits by a store man to be placed in the boat, and as he was doing so Mr McElroy asked him if he understood anything about lifeboats. When he replied that he knew a little, he was told to stay in the boat to help with the rowing. Botswain's Mate Albert Haines was put in charge, and Able Seaman George McGough took the tiller. William Ward, who was known as George, had been at sea for over twenty years, and had survived five previous shipwrecks.

As the crew were helping women to get into lifeboat 9, some of them remembered that as an older woman reached out her hand to James Widgery to be helped aboard, she became frightened and absolutely refused to get in before disappearing back into the ship. This may have been Marian Meanwell.

Marian Meanwell-Costin was a 63-year-old milliner who had crossed the Atlantic a few times previously to visit her widowed daughter and two young grandchildren. On this occasion, she intended to stay and look after the children while her daughter was at work as a dancer in a circus. She had been twice married and divorced. She had been due to take the ship *Majestic*, but on her arrival at Southampton she was told the liner was unable to sail and that she would have to travel instead on *Titanic*. She paid £8 1s for her third-class ticket. She sent a letter from Queenstown to her cousin in Cumbria, stating: 'I am delighted with *Titanic*. In my view, nothing approaching the accommodation has been experienced in any of the previous journeys and nothing but a pleasant voyage is anticipated.' She told fellow passengers that her daughter had been a very talented ballet dancer, and the audiences at the circus where she performed loved her.

Officer Moody was a tall, 24-year-old single man, who was the youngest of the officers. He had joined White Star Line in August 1911 and had served aboard RMS *Oceanic II.* He was feeling somewhat peeved, however, and had been reluctant to accept the *Titanic* assignment. Having endured a harsh winter, he was hoping to be allowed to take some time off, but his request for leave had not been granted.

One thing that may have made passengers uneasy, had they known, was the fact that there were at least two crew members on board who had been to prison for taking the life of another, and one of them, George Francis 'Paddy' McGough was in lifeboat 9. He was an able seaman working on *Titanic* as a deck hand, virtually brushing shoulders with the passengers. In 1900 he had been convicted of manslaughter on the high seas after getting drunk and causing a fellow seaman on the collier vessel *Rustington* to fall to his death in the hold of the ship while it was moored at Santos in Brazil.

The other ex-con was William Mintram, who had been convicted of manslaughter in 1902 after he had returned to his home in Southampton on a drunken rage and assaulted and stabbed his own wife in the back, causing her death. However, Mintram went down with the ship after giving his lifejacket to his son-in-law (see collapsible lifeboat B).

By this time the front of the ship was getting visibly low in the water and people were beginning to suspect that it could indeed sink. Consequently, they were becoming less reluctant to stay on board. Lifeboat 9 was still only half-filled, but things were about to change drastically.

As it was dropped down to the level of the deck, a sailor apparently came along, threw a bag into the boat, and as he climbed aboard he stated that he had been sent by the captain to take charge of the lifeboat. However, Albert Haines called his bluff and ordered him to get back out at once.

Canadian Steward William Ryerson served with the Royal Canadian Dragoons during the Boer War and later joined the British Army. Meanwhile, Quartermaster William 'Punch' Wynn had served in the Spanish-American War of 1898, and in the Boer War on transport ships.

Ninette Aubart and her maid Emma Saegesser had felt the collision and went to warn Ben Guggenheim and his valet. After Steward Etches helped Mr Guggenheim and Victor to put on their lifejackets, they all went up to the boat deck, where Mr Etches made his way towards lifeboat 5 at the front of the ship. Ninette had left £4,000 in her cabin, along with several trunks of dresses and hats she had bought in Paris. Emma got into lifeboat 9 and Ninette followed, having witnessed the way all the crew were standing around smoking and chatting, seemingly not particularly concerned about the peril they were in. As Mr Guggenheim was standing on the deck, he called out in Swiss, 'We will soon see each other again. Tomorrow *Titanic* will go on again.'

When Ninette was on board *Carpathia*, she sent a marconigram to Paris stating: 'I'm saved, but Ben lost.' She later made a claim for her losses, and in 1937 Emma Arnold Saegesser gave an interview to a Swiss radio programme, the audio for which has been preserved.

Elizabeth and Mary Lines had become alarmed when they noticed that the ship's engines had stopped to be replaced by an even louder hissing noise as steam was being released somewhere. They had only managed to get half-dressed when they were told to leave their cabin. When they ventured up to the boat deck an officer helped them to put on lifejackets (presumably Sixth Officer Moody), who tried to calm them by stating, 'We are sending you out as a matter of precaution. We hope you will be back by breakfast.' This was not particularly reassuring as it meant that they might be out on the sea in the cold air in a small boat all night!

American couple Jacques 'Jack' and Lily May Futrelle were returning from Europe as first-class passengers. Jacques was a successful writer of detective fiction and science fiction. On the night before they sailed to Southampton to board *Titanic*, they had a late-night party in London to celebrate Mr Futrelle's birthday. In the morning, they travelled to Southampton without sleeping, and Mrs Futrelle later stated that she wished he had got too drunk to travel so they would have missed the ship, and he would still be alive.

On the night of the sinking Lily went up to the boat deck where she encountered a group of men with blackened faces, who stared at her as she walked by. She remembered that they said nothing, but their eyes seemed to say, 'at least you have a chance, we have none.' Jacques refused to board a lifeboat and insisted that Lily was to take a place in lifeboat 9. The last she saw of him he was smoking a cigarette on deck with John Jacob Astor.

Jack Futrelle was lost in the sinking and May claimed £60,000 for his death. His mother died a few months after him, her death being attributed to grief over her son. His great-grandson is the writer David Futrelle.

George Brereton, known as George Brayton on *Titanic,* was one of several dodgy characters on the ship. He was an American gambler and fraudster, who embarked at Southampton as a first-class passenger. He was known to have been in the first-class smoking room stalking a victim when the collision occurred. He was rescued in lifeboat 9 and when he reached New York, he tried to fleece fellow survivor Charles Stengel in a horse racing scam. He became a car salesman in Los Angeles and committed suicide in 1942.

LIFEBOAT 11

After launching lifeboat 9, First Officer Murdoch and Sixth Officer Moody moved on to deal with lifeboat 11, which they launched at 1:20am. The craft was lowered to A Deck, and First Officer Murdoch ordered that the women and children should be taken down to that deck, where they were helped into the boat. First Officer Murdoch asked if there was a sailor in the boat, and when it was realised that there was none, Able Seaman Walter Brice jumped out and grabbed a rope and slid down into the boat, and Quartermaster Sidney Humphries was placed in charge.

When the lifeboat reached the water, the crew struggled to release the craft from its falls. To add to the problem, they were close to a condenser exhaust which was pouring out a large volume of water. They eventually released the falls and rowed away.

Stewardess Sarah Stap was the daughter of a former captain of Brunel's SS *Great Britain*, and she had actually been born on board one of his ships. She had been in bed when the collision occurred. She did not think much of it because she had been used to ships bumping before, and after asking a night watchman what had happened, he replied, 'Oh, we have only touched a bit of ice. I think it is alright. I don't think it is anything.' Because of his remarks, she remained in her cabin for a further forty-five minutes.

When she realised that there was an emergency, she went up to the boat deck and saw that the lifeboats had already been slung out. She was told to get into lifeboat 11, but on seeing a young cabin boy standing nearby, she said to him that as she was into her thirties and had had her life, he should take her seat (she was actually aged 47). The cabin boy bravely picked her up and helped her into the boat. She took charge of a baby, which she nursed for several hours, stating that it was bitterly cold and that everyone was nearly starved as they were all huddled together to try to keep warm. She remembered, 'The shrieks of the dying were positively awful.'

She later stated that Mr Ismay worked hard to get the passengers into the lifeboats, and that more lives would have been saved if people could have been persuaded to get into the boats more quickly. She also praised the bravery of the band, which were not asked to carry on playing, but 'did it absolutely on their own initiative.'

Annie Caton and Maude Slocombe were two of the five Turkish bath attendants, who received £4 a month for their wages. Men received £6 10s 2d. When Mrs Slocombe signed in to *Titanic*, she noticed that the various parts of the ship were in a semi-completed condition, with half-eaten sandwiches left in corners. After the collision they were told to get dressed and go up on deck. Miss Caton was met by an officer who re-adjusted her lifebelt, and Mrs Slocombe tried to return to her cabin to collect some possessions when she was stopped by rising water. They got together again on the boat deck and got into lifeboat 11. The three male Turkish bath attendants, John Crosbie, Walter Ennis and Leonard Taylor, lost their lives in the sinking.

Miss Caton moved to Australia where she left several accounts of her experiences:

> Well, we then drifted on and on, tossing up and down, and I cannot say how thankful we were when daylight came. After about eight hours we sighted the Carpathia and made for it, and when they picked us up we were in a half-frozen condition. The doctors attended to us all and rubbed a little life into our limbs, and wrapped us up in blankets and also gave us brandy. Everybody was very kind, but it was most awful to see the poor women crying out for husbands, sons, fathers and brothers who never came. Every man was in tears. It was heart-rending. I pray to God I may never witness such another scene.

Saloon Steward Alexander Littlejohn saw 2 feet of ice in the scuppers (the water drains) in the starboard side of the forward well deck. After helping to get about thirty-five women into lifeboat 11, and a few male first-class passengers, he and another crew member were asked by an officer to get into the boat to help to row it. The trauma of the disaster caused his hair to turn white not long afterwards, and he refused to talk about it for the rest of his life.

Edith Rosenbaum was the American fashion designer for *Women's Wear Weekly*, who had been injured in a car accident in France in the previous year in which her fiancé lost his life. She had boarded at Cherbourg after attending fashion assignments in Europe, where she had stated as she approached the massive vessel on the tender, 'I am afraid of this ship,' and she considered the atmosphere on the ship to

RMS *Titanic* set sail from Belfast for her delivery trip to Southampton. The picture shows the starboard side at the front where she collided with the iceberg. It scraped along the side and caused a series of gashes or punctures around 23 square feet in size, which were dotted along about 300 feet of the side of the ship. Lifeboats 3, 5 and 7 can be seen at the front of the boat deck with the emergency lifeboat 1 situated higher than the other three. Lifeboats 9, 11, 13 and 15 can be seen at the rear.

A view looking towards the portside rear of *Titanic*, with many people standing on the raised poop deck. Lifeboats 10, 12, 14 and 16 are clearly visible.

A view of *Titanic's* boat deck. As there is no emergency lifeboat visible in this section, it seems to be looking to the front of the ship from the starboard rear, and the lifeboats on the right of the picture are numbers 9, 11, 13 and 15.

Several people are pictured walking along the second-class promenade of the boat deck towards the portside rear of the ship. As there is land in the distance, the photograph is likely to have been taken at Queenstown. They are not taking much notice of lifeboats 10, 12, 14 and 16 visible to the left of the picture, which would be salvation for over 700 of them less than a week later. Lifeboats 2, 4 and 6 can be seen in the distance; with emergency lifeboat 2 just beyond them. It gives a good close-up look at the pulleys and ropes that worked the davits. Note the engineers and crew congregating in their promenade area.

A detailed view of the decks on RMS *Olympic,* which was the sister ship identical to RMS *Titanic.*

A depiction of the scene on the boat deck during the evacuation, which was produced by the Italian artist Fortunino Matania for the *Sphere* newspaper soon after the disaster.

It was a frightening situation for the passengers as the lifeboats descended in stops and starts before they reached the water. Washington Dodge helped his wife and son into their lifeboat, but as he looked over the side and saw the 90-feet drop, he became 'overwhelmed with doubts' that he may have put them in more danger than they would have been if they had stayed on the ship. The scene depicts the situation when lifeboat 15 nearly came down on lifeboat 13, but by this time the liner would have been further down in the water.

Men, and some women, who manned the lifeboats rowed with all their strength to get as far away as they could from the stricken liner for fear of being sucked down into the depths with her as she sank.

CS *Carpathia* was on its way from New York to Gibraltar and fortunately was in the region. After receiving distress signals from *Titanic*, it immediately set a course towards the disaster area. Working through dangerous ice fields, it arrived at the scene of devastation at four o'clock on the morning of 15 April 1912, where she rescued over 700 survivors.

Quartermaster Robert Hichens is seen guiding lifeboat 6 over choppy water towards *Carpathia*. It was the first vessel to be launched successfully from the front portside of the ship, at about one o'clock. There were several very strong personalities in the boat and there was a great deal of bad feeling among them. It reached CS *Carpathia* at seven o'clock.

Lifeboat 14 under the command of Fifth Officer Harold Lowe as it approached *Carpathia*, with Collapsible D in tow. The picture gives a good impression of how isolated they must have felt in the vastness of the sea.

Collapsible D was the last lifeboat to be launched from *Titanic*, about fifteen minutes before the ship went down. The craft contained the Navratil 'Titanic orphans', and Richard Williams, who nearly lost his legs but recovered to go on to win an Olympic gold medal at the 'Chariots of Fire' Games.

Lifeboat 11 arrives at the side of *Carpathia* at about seven o'clock, with Quartermaster Sidney Humphreys in charge. After spending several hours freezing on the open sea, they were faced with the task of climbing a precarious rope ladder. The passengers included Edith Rosenbaum with her toy pig.

Titanic's lifeboats gathered at Pier 54 in New York. Crew member Edward Tufts stated in the *Evening World* newspaper that although eighteen boats reached *Carpathia*, 'Thirteen of these boats were brought in on *Carpathia's* davits, while five were cast adrift at sea because there was no room for them.' It is not known what happened to most of them afterwards, but it is believed they were distributed among other White Star liners, particularly her sister ship RMS *Olympic*.

The Collapsible B raft slid off the deck and was floating upside down in the water. As many as thirty people were stood on its hull as it drifted for several hours before they were transferred to another lifeboat. It was found adrift in the ocean by men from the rescue ship CS *Mackay-Bennett* on 20 April.

Collapsible A was washed off the boat deck as *Titanic* went down. RMS *Oceanic* found it on 13 May, containing three decomposed bodies. They also found an inscribed ring, which is believed to have belonged to a Swedish couple who had died during the evacuation.

be cold and impersonal. She wrote from Queenstown to her secretary in Paris: 'I am going to take my very much needed rest on this trip, but I cannot get over my feeling of depression and premonition of trouble.'

In addition to her own first-class cabin in A11 on the starboard front end of the ship, she is believed to have reserved room E63 for the nineteen trunks containing fashion items she was eager to take back to New York. It would seem that Edith had made enquiries about insuring her luggage but had been told quite confidently that there was no need to waste her money because the ship was 'unsinkable'.

After her near-fatal car crash her mother had given Edith a French symbol of luck in the shape of a papier-mâché music box pig, which played a French song when the tail was wound. She was of the opinion that the tune was 'The Maxixe' (a style of Brazilian tango), but the Maritime Museum at Greenwich believe it to be entitled 'La Sorella' ('The Sister'). Her mother had told her to keep it with her at all times so, as she had left it in her cabin, her room steward, a Liverpudlian named Robert Wareham, went back to get it for her. When he returned, he informed her that it was below her cabin where the ship had been pierced by the iceberg. As she was sat in the A deck lounge, she sensed the situation becoming more serious, so she handed her trunk keys to Wareham for him to go and check on them, to which he responded, 'Now, if I were you, I think I would go back to your room and kiss them goodbye.' Steward Wareham lost his life in the sinking, leaving a wife and five young children.

Probably still convinced that the ship was unsinkable, someone suggested a snowball fight on deck, before realising it was too cold. Edith had decided not to get into a lifeboat and leave her belongings behind. However, as her cherished pig was wrapped in a blanket, a member of the crew thought she was carrying a baby under her arms and he took it from her and threw it into the crowded lifeboat 11, damaging a leg, and she was compelled to follow it.

In her written accounts she says that in the lifeboat there were 'seven babies... perpetually crying,' but she does not mention until her BBC interview in 1956 that she actually played the music box's tune to try to soothe them. It came into the possession of the *Titanic* expert Walter Lord and is now at the National Maritime Museum in Greenwich, London. A fellow passenger in the lifeboat complained to some of the officers that there was a real pig in the boat.

One of the crying babies was likely to have been 11-month-old Hudson Trevor Allison, who was accompanied by his nursemaid Alice Cleaver. Alice had brought the child to lifeboat 11, where she handed him to Bedroom Steward William Faulkner while she got into the boat.

When the officers saw him holding an infant, he too was told to get on board.

Alice Cleaver, who had worked for wealthy English families from her teen years, was in the employ of Hudson 'Hud' Allison and his wife Bess. Their 2-year-old daughter Loraine and 1-year-old son Hudson Trevor were also travelling with them on the ship. London-born Sarah Daniels was the personal maid to Mrs Allison, and George Swane from Brighton was employed as their chauffeur. They also employed a cook named Amelia 'Mildred' Brown, who shared second-class cabin F33 with Elizabeth Nye from Kent, Mrs Amelia Lemore, and Selina Cook, who was on her way to visit her mother in New York and was suffering from toothache.

Hud Allison was a wealthy Montreal stockbroker who had purchased first-class cabins C22, 24 and 26 for the journey back to Canada. Mr and Mrs Allison shared one cabin, Sarah Daniels and Loraine shared another, and Alice and Hudson Trevor shared the third. Officially Hud was in England to attend a business meeting, but as devout Methodists, they had Hudson Trevor baptised at Epworth Church in Lincolnshire, where the Methodist founder John Wesley had lived and preached. They purchased furniture for a new home and went up to Scotland to buy several horses for their stock farm. They also recruited the four members of staff for their two new residences.

Mr and Mrs Allison were dining companions of Major Peuchen, and a fellow Canadian named Harry Molson. After *Titanic* hit the iceberg, Hud went up on deck to find out what had happened, while Alice picked up Trevor and went to collect the rest of the servants in second class. Hud returned to find their cabin empty. He took Bess and Loraine up to the boat deck and, seeing Major Peuchen in lifeboat 6, he helped them to get on board, and then went away to try to find his son.

In the meantime, George Swane had accompanied Alice Cleaver, Hudson Trevor, Mildred Brown and Elizabeth Nye to the boat deck and got them into lifeboat 11. Sarah Daniels had already gone up to the boat deck to investigate and was placed into lifeboat 8 by a steward, who promised to inform the Allisons of her whereabouts.

Major Peuchen believed Mrs Allison and Loraine could have got away in lifeboat 6, but somebody told Mrs Allison that her husband was in a boat on the opposite side of the deck (portside), so she grabbed Loraine, climbed out of the lifeboat and rushed away. Apparently, when she got to the other side of the ship, she could not find her husband, by which time lifeboat 6 had departed. Mr and Mrs Allison and George Swane lost their lives in the sinking, as did Loraine, the only child from the first- and second-class passengers who did not survive.

Janie Quick was a native of Plymouth in Devon, who had boarded *Titanic* at Southampton with her two daughters, 8-year-old Winifred and 2-year-old Phyllis. She and her husband Frederick had recently moved to start a new life in Detroit, and she had returned to Plymouth to visit family. Janie did not think much of it when she was awakened by the collision, but when some crewmen alerted her to the seriousness of the situation, she woke the girls and got them ready. She struggled up towards A Deck, carrying Phyllis wrapped in a shawl and holding Winifred with the other hand. At the staircase she was helped by some passengers to put a lifejacket on Phyllis, which freed her to put on her own.

As Henry Morley and Kate Phillips left their cabin, Henry quickly put the 'Love of the Ocean' pendant around Kate's neck. When they got to the starboard rear of the boat deck, Kate was offered a place in lifeboat 11. Henry tried to cling on to her arm, but a member of the crew took hold of her and pulled her away from him. The craft was lowered and rowed away from the liner, and soon afterwards one of the sailors noticed she was only scantily clad and so wrapped his jumper around her to try to keep her warm.

LIFEBOAT 13

Ten minutes later, at about 1:30am, First Officer Murdoch and Sixth Officer Moody moved quickly on to prepare lifeboat 13 for launching. Leading fireman Fred Barrett was placed in charge and Lookout Reg Lee was also on board, as was a first-class dining room steward named Frederick Dent Ray, who had served in the 1899–1902 Anglo-Boer War with the Cape Mounted Police.

Fred Ray had been re-directed from RMS *Olympic* to RMS *Titanic,* where he shared room 3 in E Deck with twenty-seven other crew members. He had come off duty at 9pm on the night of the collision and was asleep when two fellow stewards came and told him he was to go with them to the lifeboats. After assisting at lifeboats 9 and 11, he got into lifeboat 13. As the craft was being lowered down to the water, an infant wrapped in a blanket was thrown down to him, which he caught and kept alive until being rescued. He stated that when he ran up to A Deck, there was only two boats left. Lifeboat 13 was nearly full when he got in, and even more people clambered in after him, and he heard someone shout from the boat deck above, 'Let no more in that boat. The falls will break.'

Lawrence Beesley had been reading in his D56 cabin from 11:15pm, to the time when the vessel struck. He particularly noticed an increased vibration during this period and assumed that the speed was higher than at any previous time during the day. At 11:45pm an extra heave of the engines aroused his curiosity. On going to investigate, he found himself at the starboard rear of the ship at about 12:20am, where he saw crewmen busy preparing the lifeboats in that area of the ship. 'We watched the crew at work on the lifeboats, numbers 9, 11, 13 and 15, some inside arranging the oars, some coiling ropes on the deck – the ropes which ran through the pulleys to lower the lifeboats to the sea – others with cranks fitted to the rocking arms of the davits. As we watched, the cranks were turned, the davits swung outwards until the boats hung clear of the edge of the deck.'

A sailor asked Mr Beesley if there were any more ladies on his deck, and there being none, invited him to jump in. He later remembered noticing that there were no officers in the boat, and no one seemed to know what to do. The boat was swung under the descending lifeboat 15, but a stoker in Mr Beesley's boat cut her away, thus preventing the other boat from falling on and crushing her. The stoker then took charge of the boat. Mr Beesley wrote a successful book about his experiences, *The Loss of the SS* Titanic: *Its Story and Its Lessons*, which was published only nine weeks after the disaster.

An Irish girl named Bridget McDermott had boarded the ship with some apprehension. Her niece had reported that on the evening before she left for Queenstown, a little man in black had tapped Bridget on the shoulder and told her that he knew she was going on a long journey and, 'There will be a tragedy but you will be saved.' He suddenly disappeared and nobody around her saw the man, only Bridget. She had brought a new stylish hat which she was very fond of and when she got into the lifeboat, she realised that she had left it in her cabin. She clambered back out of the lifeboat, ran all the way back to her cabin to retrieve it, then ran back to the open deck and jumped 15 feet from a rope ladder onto the lifeboat.

Daniel Buckley, an Irish third-class passenger who was going to America with a group of cousins and friends, had forced his way through a locked gate to get to the top deck. He stated at the United States Senate inquiry that when he got there, he helped to put women and children into a number of lifeboats, and when he got to lifeboat 13, he decided to jump in with several other men. The officers in charge of the craft ordered them all to get back out, which most of them did, but a female passenger took pity on Daniel and threw a shawl over him and pushed him down to hide him at the bottom of the boat. He was killed in action during the First World War.

Ellen Shine, an Irish woman from third class, who was going across the Atlantic to be with her brother in New York, stated in the *Brooklyn Daily Eagle*:

> Those who were able to get out of bed rushed to the upper deck where they were met by members of the crew who were trying to keep them in the steerage quarters. The women, however, rushed past the men, pushing them down, and finally reached the upper deck. When they were informed that the boat was sinking, most of them fell on their knees and began to pray. I saw one of the lifeboats and made for it. There were already four men in it from steerage. They were ordered out by an officer but they refused to leave. Then one of the officers jumped into the boat

> and drawing a revolver he shot them dead. Their bodies were picked out from the bottom of the boat and thrown into the water.

Ellen was the last living survivor who came from an Irish background.

Elizabeth Dowdell had just put her 6-year-old charge Virginia to bed when someone came running along the passage shouting, 'All hands dress and put on lifebelts.' When they tried to get on deck the stairways were crowded. Men and women were climbing over each other, 'and their cries and curses were terrible to hear.' Seeing their plight, a member of the crew picked Virginia up and tried to lift her up to other crew members reaching down from the gallery above. The little girl was too small, so he asked her to step on his face to get a bit higher, which she did, and was lifted up. The man then assisted Elizabeth and wished her good luck.

They were assisted to get into lifeboat 13 and Elizabeth stated later, 'Several men tried to rush in on us before we were lowered. I saw an officer shoot three of them. The others stopped immediately.' Officer Murdoch had a gun. She stated that many people who were swimming around near the lifeboat were brought on board. When they were on board *Carpathia,* they met up with their room-mate Amy Stanley, who had been rescued in lifeboat 15, which had nearly come down on top of them.

Warsaw-born Leah Aks and her 10-month-old son Philip (known as Filly) were third-class passengers on their way to America, where her husband Sam had settled as a scrap metal dealer. He too was Warsaw-born and had never met his son. Leah and Filly had been booked onto an earlier trip, but her mother had convinced her to wait a few days and travel instead on the 'unsinkable' *Titanic.*

Almost an hour after the collision, the two had to be carried past people blocking the third-class metal staircase up to the boat deck. When they got there, Madeleine Astor covered Filly's head with her shawl to try to keep him warm. However, a disgruntled man who had been refused entry into a lifeboat and did not agree with the drill, shouted, 'I'll show you women and children first!' and snatched Filly from Liah's arms, callously throwing him over the railing. Fortunately, he landed in the arms of someone in the number 11 lifeboat, which was just being launched. Before Leah had chance to realise what had happened, she was urged into lifeboat 13.

As the boat was being lowered, some of the occupants had to push it away from the side of the ship to avoid an outfall of water gushing from a vent. When it reached the water, Fred Barrett was alarmed to see that as lifeboat 15 was coming down, lifeboat 13 was drifting under it, and he had to work fast to cut it free from the falls and steer it away. This was not made easy by the fact that it was so full of people, the weight had forced the sides of the boat to sink within a few inches of the water.

Leah Aks spent the night in utter distress until the arrival of *Carpathia*, and as soon as she got on the rescue ship, she searched the deck in desperation for Filly, without success. Feeling despondent, she lay on a mattress on one of the lower decks for two days. A woman named Selena Cook became concerned for her and prompted her to go up on deck to take in some fresh air, and when she did, she heard Filly crying and they were re-united.

Ruth Becker was just 12 years old, and her father was a Lutheran pastor working as a missionary in India. She had been returning from India to the United States with her mother Elizabeth, known as 'Nella', her sister Maria and her brother Richard, who had fallen ill and prompted them to have to return to America, where Indian physicians had advised he would stand more chance of recovery.

After the collision, the four of them were waiting on the boat deck when Mrs Becker became concerned at how cold it was and asked Ruth to go back to their cabin to get some blankets. As she got back to the boat deck, her two siblings were put into lifeboat 11, and her mother was forced to follow them, shouting back to Ruth to get into the next lifeboat, number 13, which she did without any fuss. She was reunited with her family on *Carpathia* later that day.

Fred Barrett was only wearing light clothing designed to work in the hot boiler rooms and he became too cold to continue helping. A woman put a shawl around his shoulders and he fell asleep until the lifeboat was brought safely to the side of the *Carpathia* at 4:45am; the first regular lifeboat to reach the rescue ship.

LIFEBOAT 15

It would seem that only five minutes had elapsed before First Officer Murdoch and Sixth Officer Moody had moved quickly on from lifeboat 13 to prepare lifeboat 15 for launching; the fourth and final lifeboat at the starboard rear of the ship. This was the fourth lifeboat the same two officers had prepared and launched together and by this time they must have been tired and feeling the strain.

Frank Dymond was a West Country man. During his service in the Royal Navy from 1897 to 1904, he had spent numerous times in cells for misconduct. He was a good boxer, and his family described him as a 'hard man'. He was working as a fireman on the ship and had been on his way to start his shift when he discovered that the door to the boiler room was shut and the stairwell was flooded. He was assigned to lifeboat 15, but when he got up to the starboard rear of the boat deck, he saw that lifeboats 13 and 15 had already been prepared for launching, and he was told to get into lifeboat 15, and ordered to take charge.

As the craft reached A Deck it stopped to take on more people, but there was a rush to try to get into the boat and he had to strike a 'foreigner' who had clambered on board. As it was lowered further, he remembered that the lifeboat was damaged as it kept banging into the side of the ship. Several men fell from the craft into the sea, and when it reached the water Frank took the tiller to guide it away from the ship.

There is believed to have been as many as sixty-eight people in the boat, including three men who had seen active service in the 1899–1902 Anglo-Boer War. Fireman William Clark had served with Brabant's Horse under Lord Methuen; Third Class Steward Arthur Ernest Read Lewis had served as a teenager on a hospital ship; and Third Class Steward John Edward Hart, had served with the South African Light Horse during the operations in the relief of Ladysmith. Steward Hart had gathered together a group of about twenty-five third-class women and children and escorted them up to the boat deck, where they were found spaces in lifeboat 15.

Bridget Moran, sometimes known as Bertha, was travelling with her brother Daniel. They were Irish but had moved to live in New York where Daniel had become a police officer. Their father had recently died, and they had received some inheritance which Daniel carried on his person in the form of banknotes. Also in their party was Patrick Ryan and Margaret Madigan, with Patrick stating that he was travelling to New York with the possibility of employment with the New York Police Department. They had boarded at Queenstown and Bertha and Margaret shared a cabin in second class.

Bertha had felt a jolt at the time of the collision, and, after throwing a coat over her night clothes, she and all her party made their way towards the upper deck. There, they found that some members of the crew were stopping people from getting to A Deck, from where the rear lifeboats were being loaded. They eventually arrived at lifeboat 15, where Father Thomas Byles assisted Martha and Margaret to board. As Daniel and Patrick stood by, Daniel tried to reassure Bridget by telling her not to fear for him.

Alina Johnson, original from Finland and usually known as Alice, had been living in America with her husband Oscar, when she heard that her father was ill and returned to Scandinavia to look after him. After his death she bought tickets for the return home on *Titanic*. Oscar had refurbished their home as a surprise welcome home.

She was travelling as a third-class passenger with her 4-year-old son Harold and 8-month-old daughter Eleanor. They shared a cabin with two Swedish ladies named Elin Braf, 20, and Helmina Nilsson, 26, who was rescued in lifeboat 13. Shortly after the collision, Alice and Elin went out on deck and were kicking around pieces of ice that had fallen off the iceberg, when an officer told them to get back to their cabins as a ship would be on its way soon. Not long afterwards a steward came to help them. He had taken a liking to them as he had waited on them in the third-class dining room, and, with a group of fellow Swedes, he is believed to have led them to lifeboat 15 on the starboard rear of the boat deck. Alice was helped into the boat with Eleanor in her arms, and called to Elin to get in with Harold, but she remained rigid in fear on deck, so a crewman took Harold from her and threw him into the boat. Alice continued to try to persuade Elin to get into the boat but without success, and she lost her life.

Another Swedish couple named Carl and Selma Asplund had boarded the ship at Southampton as third-class passengers travelling to America, with their 5-year-old twins Lilian and Carl Edgar, and three other sons named Filip (13), Clarence (9) and Edvin (3). Lilian remembered that she did not like the smell of fresh paint when they boarded the ship. There was another set of twins on *Titanic,* who were identical, named Kate and Alice Herman, aged 24.

After the collision the family got to the first-class promenade window on A Deck, where Lilian, along with the twins and Edvin, were loaded into lifeboat 10 by Carl, despite Selma's wishes that she wanted to remain with Carl, stating that she would rather remain with him and go down with the ship. However, Carl made the point that the children should not be alone, and Selma was practically thrown into the boat. Because the lifeboat was full, there was no more room for the other boys, and Carl assured her, 'Go ahead, we will get into one of the other boats.' They stood at the rail for a while, and then Carl led Filip and Clarence away to their fate.

Selma was haunted by the memory of that scene, but she kept Edvin on her lap and Lilian between her legs, hoping that she could keep them warm that way. All their clothes had become dirty and wet by the time they were taken on board *Carpathia.* A woman took off the twins' clothes and dried them, but to add to Selma's distress, they had become separated for a while. When they were re-united, they were taken to the sick bay. Lilian recalled, 'The people on *Carpathia* were very good to us.' She was one of the last people to survive the sinking who actually had memories of the incident.

It is not known for certain on which lifeboat the Herman twins and their mother escaped. Their parents were Samuel and Jane, and the family lived in Somerset, where Samuel ran a hotel. They were on their way to New Jersey to be with Jane's brother, and they boarded *Titanic* at Southampton. With them was a teenager named George Sweet, who worked for Samuel, and who was in their care. They were anticipating George's fifteenth birthday on the following Tuesday. They should have travelled on an earlier ship, but they fatefully cancelled to give them more time to prepare. Jane had only put on light clothing and suffered terribly from the cold while in 'the second lifeboat launched'. Samuel and George Sweet were lost at sea.

Harry Homer, listed as E Haven on *Titanic,* was another confidence trickster and card sharp who embarked at Southampton, and was rescued in lifeboat 15. Lucy Duff-Gordon remembered that she had seen Homer dealing from the bottom of a deck of cards. He kept up his card sharp lifestyle after the disaster, on various transatlantic liners. He was frequently arrested and jailed for breaking various laws before his death in 1939.

Note: Charles Romaine was yet another dodgy character who used a number of aliases and was remembered as one of several passengers engaged in gambling on the ship. He survived the sinking, but it is not certain in which lifeboat. In later life he went straight as a stockbroker, but he was hit by a New York taxi in January 1922 and died of his injuries.

As his boat was being lowered, Fireman Dymond saw that lifeboat 13 was still under tension and had drifted back towards the ship, right underneath him. He shouted back up to the officers on deck to stop lowering, but he was not heard. Fortunately, the crew of lifeboat 13 managed to cut it free just in time. Lifeboat 15 was one of the very last to be picked up by *Carpathia*.

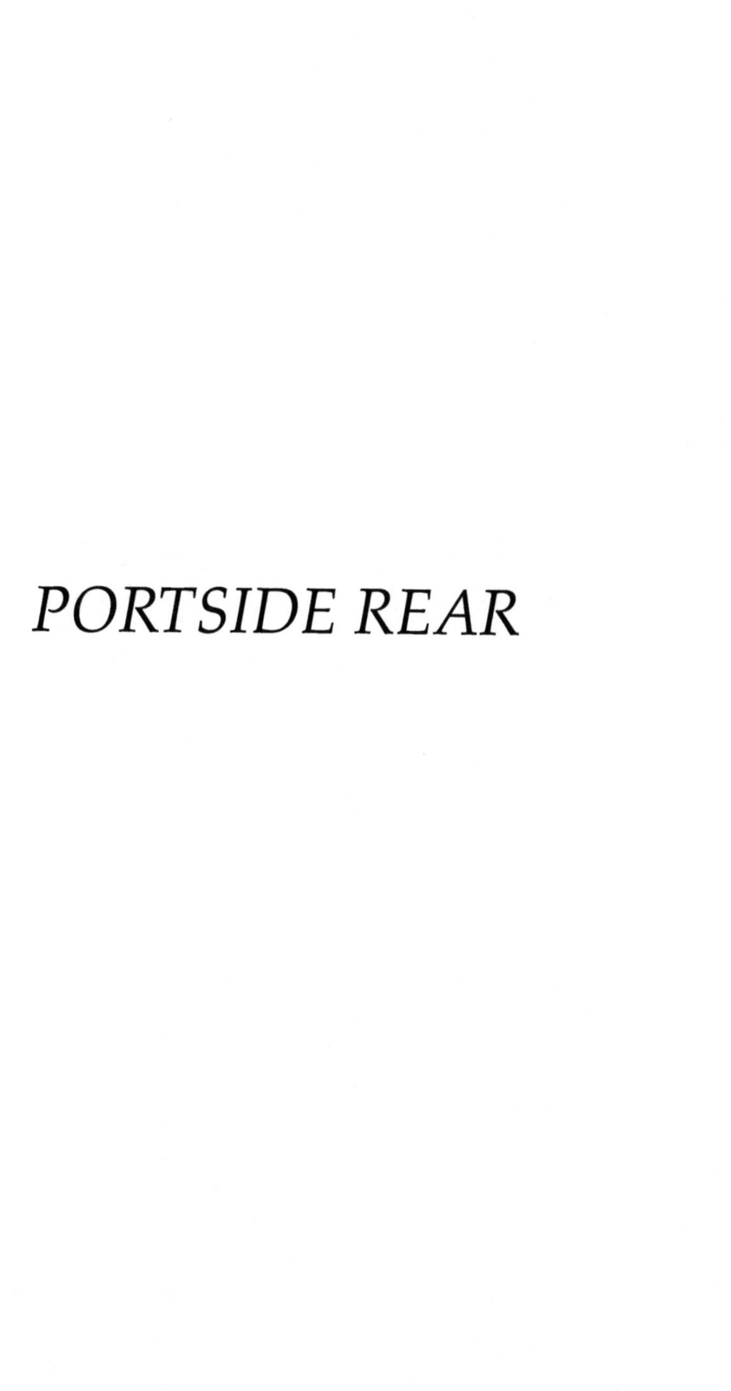

PORTSIDE REAR

LIFEBOAT 16

From about 1:20am Chief Officer Wilde, Second Officer Lightoller, Fifth Officer Lowe and Sixth Officer Moody began working on lifeboats 10, 12, 14 and 16 at the rear of the ship on the left (port) side, which had become the danger zone, as passengers and some of the crew had realised *Titanic* was going down and their chances of survival were slim. It must have crossed their minds by this time that some areas in the depth of the ship must have been completely filled with water, and the dreadful thought hit them that without doubt there had to be some instances of people having drowned. Master-at-Arms Joseph Bailey was placed in charge, along with Seamen Ernest Archer and James Forward.

Joseph 'Job' Bailey had served with the Royal Navy from 1880 to 1903, but *Titanic* was his first ship of a merchant fleet. The only other master-at-arms in the ship was Thomas Walter King. The duty of a master-at-arms is to act as a law enforcement officer and supervise security.

Second Officer Lightoller recorded:

> Between one boat being lowered away and the next boat being prepared, I usually nipped along to have a look down the very long emergency staircase leading direct from the boat deck down to C deck. Actually built as a short cut for the crew, it served my purpose now to gauge the speed with which the water was rising, and how high it had got. By now the foredeck was below the surface. That cold, green water crawling its ghostly way up that staircase was a sight that stamped itself indelibly on my memory. Step by step it made its way up, covering the electric lights, one after the other, which, for a time, shone under the surface with a terrible weird effect.

Lizzie Wilkinson remembered that she was asleep at the time of the collision but was awakened by the shock. When she rushed up to the boat deck, she was ordered into a lifeboat but feared to trust herself in one of the frail craft. While officers with drawn revolvers issued their orders, one of the men forced her bodily into lifeboat 16.

Charles Andrews was an award-winning swimmer from Liverpool, who had been on RMS *Olympic* when it collided with HMS *Hawke* and was working as a saloon steward. His cousin, George Roberton, was also a steward, and they were both aged 19. He saw stores being brought to the boat including bread, but he did not see any put into the boat.

He helped a number of women and children into the lifeboat and then stood back. As the boat was about to be lowered, an officer looked around and asked Charles if he could take an oar, and on telling the officer that he could, he was ordered into the boat. His cousin was lost in the sinking.

Upon settling down in her bunk, Violet Jessop found the prayer she had with her and read it. Then she made Elizabeth Leather read it too. Soon afterwards Violet was 'comfortably drowsy' but not quite asleep when the collision happened. She and Elizabeth were ordered up on deck, apparently being told to serve as an example of how to behave for the non-English speakers, who were struggling to comprehend the instructions given to them.

She remembered, 'I was ordered up on deck. Calmly, passengers strolled about. I stood at the bulkhead with the other stewardesses, watching the women cling to their husbands before being put into the boats with their children. Sometime after, a ship's officer [Sixth Officer Moody] ordered us into lifeboat 16 [her and Elizabeth Leather]; first to show some women it was safe. As the boat was being lowered the officer called: "Here, Miss Jessop, look after this baby." And a bundle was dropped onto my lap.'

Violet stated that while she was on board the rescue ship, 'I was still clutching the baby against my hard cork lifebelt I was wearing when a woman leaped at me and grabbed the baby and rushed off with it. It appeared that she put it down on the deck of the *Titanic* while she went off to fetch something, and when she came back the baby had gone. I was too frozen and numb to think it strange that this woman had not stopped to say, "thank you".'

Elizabeth Leather was one of only two stewardesses to be called to give evidence at the United States Senate inquiry; the other being Annie Robinson, who was rescued in lifeboat 11.

Margaret Mannion left from Queenstown with her fiancé Martin Gallagher, her best friend Ellen Mockler and Martin's friends Thomas Kilgannon and Thomas Smyth. At 11:40pm on the night of the disaster, just as she was beginning to sleep, there was a sudden, violent jerk which threw people across their cabins. Then there was silence, and the engine stopped.

Margaret jumped out of bed and rushed out into the corridor to see what was going on, along with many of the other passengers. Suddenly, an ear-splitting siren went off and people began to panic. Just then a very loud crashing sound shook the vessel. The two girls were in a terrible state because neither they nor any of the third-class passengers knew what was going on. They became desperate when the water started to rise about their feet. The men stormed down the corridors, followed by the ladies in their light clothes. Having smashed a locked barrier, they were face with armed sailors, but they brushed them aside in their frantic desire to get to the boat deck. When they reached the deck, the second-class passengers were already climbing into the lifeboats. The sailors had no choice but to let them follow.

Miss Mannion jumped into lifeboat 16 with Ellen Mockler, who also survived. She caught a final glimpse of Martin Gallagher kneeling with a group of passengers on the deck, saying the Rosary. A first-class passenger possibly saved her life by giving her a fur coat to protect her from the cold until she was rescued by *Carpathia*. Martin Gallagher, Thomas Kilgannon and Thomas Smyth all lost their lives.

LIFEBOAT 12

Chief Officer Wilde and Second Officer Lightoller began to work on launching lifeboat 12 at about 1:25am. Able Seaman John Poingdestre, a Channel Islander, was given charge of this craft. He noticed that a large and restless crowd was beginning to gather around all the lifeboats at the rear portside, and it was becoming difficult for the officers to keep them at bay.

Able Seaman Frederick Clench had helped to uncover lifeboat 11, and he was in lifeboat 16 trying to refit the pug when the boat was swung out ready to launch. He jumped back out onto the deck, where he assisted Second Officer Lightoller and three other officers to prepare and launch lifeboat 14. When it was seen that there were not enough seamen in lifeboat 12, Able Seaman Clench was ordered to get on board. His brother George lost his life in the sinking.

Swiss teenage waitress Bertha Lehmann was travelling alone, having boarded at Cherbourg as a second-class passenger. She had been seasick for most of the voyage, and as she did not speak English, she spent most of her time reading in her cabin. Bertha Lehmann had told her brother and sister in America that she was going to visit them in May, but chose to go earlier to surprise them. After spending some time in the library writing letters, she was in bed when the ship hit the iceberg, which she described as being like a train 'grinding to a very sudden stop.' Being alarmed by two excited ladies in the next cabin, she went out into the corridor, where she met Roger Bricoux of the ship's orchestra, who advised her to put on some warm clothes as he thought the passengers were being transferred to another ship. He escorted her to lifeboat 12 and helped her to board.

Dagmar and Kurt Bryhl, along with Dagmar's fiancé Ingvar Enander, were travelling in second class on their way to visit her uncle who lived in Illinois, where Ingvar also wanted to study agriculture. Dagmar and Ingvar were planning to marry very soon. Kurt, an upholsterer by trade, went along as an interpreter, intending to remain in America.

Dagmar remembered that on the night of the sinking, Kurt had been wearing a grey-speckled costume. They had been reassured by members of the crew that there was no danger, but Ingvar had a feeling of danger, and they all went up to the boat deck. Ingvar picked up Dagmar and carried her to lifeboat 12. She tried to get the officers to allow Kurt and Ingvar to get in the lifeboat with her. She clung to them both and put her arms around them, pleading with the officers to allow them to get on board, but they would not allow it. Wearing just a coat over her night gown, she had to suffer the cold night air. Kurt and Ingvar lost their lives, and the only thing Dagmar had saved was a watch and chain Ingvar had bought for her, which she wore around her neck.

Belfast-born Mary Sloan and Evelyn Marsden had shared a cabin together, and both worked as nurse stewardesses to first-class saloon passengers. Evelyn was Australian and was described as 'one of the cleverest horsewomen in the district'. She was an accomplished telegraph operator, had trained to be a nurse, but had chosen a life at sea and was working on RMS *Olympic* when that ship collided with HMS *Hawke*. She was engaged to a ship's doctor.

After *Titanic* hit the iceberg, Evelyn and Mary were comforted by Assistant Surgeon John Simpson. He took them to his cabin and gave then a tot of whisky and water to try to calm their nerves. After they left the cabin, they did not see him again and he was lost.

The pair reached the boat deck at the portside rear of the ship. Mary was standing by lifeboat 16 when Thomas Andrews recognised her and asked why she was still there. She replied, 'All my friends are staying behind. It would be mean to go.' Mr Andrews said, 'It would be mean for you not to go. You must get in.' Miss Sloan finally assented and was aboard the boat when it left the ship.

Evelyn had learned how to row and control a boat against the tides and currents on the Murray River in Australia, and she was able to put her skills to good use as she helped to get lifeboat 16 away from *Titanic* as she went down. It is believed she also tended to a baby.

Alice Phillips was a 21-year-old West Country girl whose mother had recently passed away, so her father, Escott, had sold their house and they were on their way to Pennsylvania to live with Escott's brother. They paid £21 for their ticket, and during the voyage Alice shared a cabin with Agnes Davis and her son, John, and Maude Sincock, all of whom lived at St Ives in Cornwall. She stated:

> I was in the cabin when all at once there was a tremendous shock. Naturally I was dreadfully frightened, and at once ran outside, along

> with Mrs Davies. Just beyond the doorway I met the cabin steward and asked him what had happened? 'Everything is all right,' he said, and advised me to go back to the cabin. I was not convinced. Something felt amiss. Dad came by our room and I accompanied him to the open deck.
>
> There, we stood back and watched as sailors pulled tarps off the lifeboats. One of the crew shouted, 'All on deck with lifebelts on!' Dad and I hurried below to alert my cabin companions. With our lifejackets on, Dad and I hurried back to the upper deck. I shivered from the cold. In my haste, I'd forgotten my coat. An officer called, 'Women and children first!' Father walked me over to the lifeboat on the port side. He kissed me on my cheek and helped me into the boat. 'Don't worry,' he said. 'I'll join you later.'
>
> As the small boat lurched toward the sea, a young man jumped in. Once on the water, sailors took to the oars and pulled away from the ship. Then came what sounded like an explosion. I watched in disbelief as the *Titanic* dove into the ocean. Those left aboard were tossed into the icy sea. I could never forget their cries for help. It was awful. And to know my dear father suffered such a tragedy was too terrible to even think about. I almost felt I would have liked to have died with him.
>
> Our boat drifted along in the calm sea. There was nary a ripple. Thousands upon thousands of stars shone bright. In the bone-chilling night, we nearly froze to death. Then in mid-ocean, several of the lifeboats were tied together to help make us more visible to a rescue ship. With room in our boat, we took on more passengers from the ones that were overcrowded.

When they had been in the water for a while they encountered lifeboats 4, 10, collapsible D and 14, with Fifth Office Lowe in charge of lifeboat 14. He distributed his passengers into the other boats in the flotilla so he could go back to the wreckage to see if he could save anyone. Therefore, lifeboat 12 received several passengers from lifeboat 14, along with two or three crew members from collapsible D.

Alice Phillips lamented:

> Before the sun rose and the dark began to slip away, I glanced around at the pale, ghostlike faces of those who survived this horrible night. But how much longer could any of us last? Was a ship coming? Then a sharp sound of a whistle grabbed our attention. Across the waves, we spotted an upside-down life-raft and rowed toward her. Standing on top of the boat were men, some looking near collapse. Carefully, they balanced themselves on the bottom of the overturned boat. The survivors were assisted into our lifeboats, and still holding onto hope, I searched for my father's face. When I saw that Dad was not among them, I cried. Then

> blue lights appeared in the sky – rockets. A ship came into view. At last, we were saved!

Lifeboat 12 was the last to be rescued, at about 8am, and Alice Phillips recalled:

> Steaming through fog and a dreadful lightning storm, our rescue ship – the RMS *Carpathia* – arrived in New York on Thursday night. With the other survivors, I made my way down the gangplank. Somewhere from within the enormous crowd, I heard my name called. A man waved his arms above his head. 'Alice! Alice!' I recognised him from an old photograph. 'Uncle William?' He approached me and I dissolved into tears. 'Dad is gone. I'm afraid I shall never see my poor father again.' I collapsed into his arms and sobbed.

LIFEBOAT 14

Lifeboat 14 was launched at 1:30am from the rear portside by Chief Officer Wilde, Second Officer Lightoller, Fifth Officer Lowe and Sixth Officer Moody.

Fifth Officer Lowe was asleep at the time of the collision, and he was half awakened by hearing voices in the officers' quarters. After a short while he jumped out of bed and looked out of the door, where he saw women in the quarters with lifebelts on. These quarters were usually off-limits to passengers, so, on realising something serious was wrong, he got dressed and went out on deck. He stated that when he reached the boat deck: 'I could feel by my feet there was something wrong – it is not listing it is tipping – she was by the bow; she was very much by the bow. She had a grade downhill... by the head.' An American woman named Daisy Ida Minahan, who ended up in his lifeboat 14, stated: 'The frightful slant of the deck toward the bow of the boat gave us our first thought of danger.'

Fifth Officer Lowe saw that there was some activity on the starboard (right) side of the ship, so he joined the men working in that area. Among these men was Able Seaman Joe Scarrott, who remembered that some 'foreigners' tried to rush the boat, but he kept them at bay by swinging the tiller back and forth to stop them from getting on board.

Esther Hart's bad forebodings had become a dreadful reality. She and her daughter Eva were put into lifeboat 14, and Esther remembered:

> I know that there was a cry of: 'she's sinking!' I heard hoarse shouts of 'Women and children first,' and then from boat to boat we were hurried, only to be told 'already full.' Four boats we tried, and at the fifth there was room. Eva was thrown in first, and I followed her. Just then a man who had previously tried to get in, succeeded in doing so, but was ordered out, and the officer fired his revolver into the air to let everyone see it was loaded, and shouted out, 'Stand back, I say, Stand back. The next, man who puts his foot in this boat I will shoot him down like a dog.'

Ben Hart had been doing what he could to help the women and children. Then he stopped to address his wife and daughter. He gave his coat to Esther to keep her and Eva warm, and stated calmly, 'I'm not going in.' Then he turned to the officers and pleaded, 'For God's sake look after my wife and child.' And little Eva called out to the officer with the revolver, 'Don't shoot my daddy! You shan't shoot my daddy.'

Esther lamented:

> That was the last I saw of my poor lost dear – no farewell kiss, no fond word - but in a moment, he had gone and we were hanging over the sea, 50 or 60 feet above it, and then there were two or three horrible jerks as the boat was lowered from the davits and we were in the water, so crowded that we could scarcely move. The officer in charge of our boat was standing on that raised part of it right at the end. We were all women and children aboard (at least I thought so then, but we were not, as I will presently tell you), and we were all crying and sobbing; and the officer said, not roughly, but I think with a kindly desire to keep our minds off the terrible time we had gone through: 'Don't cry, please, don t cry. You'll have something else to do than cry; some of you will have to handle the oars. For God's sake, stop crying. If I had not the responsibility of looking after you, I would put a bullet through my brain.'

Harvey Collyer went up on deck when he realised there was a problem. On his return he reported to his wife Lottie, 'What do you think? We've struck an iceberg – a big one – but there's no danger. An officer told me.' Lottie asked if anybody seemed frightened, and when Harvey said no, she lay back again in her bunk as she was feeling a bit sick from eating the rich food they had been served that day. After they had heard a lot of people running past the door of their cabin, they all went up to the boat deck, where their daughter, 8-year-old Madge, was taken from Lottie's hands and placed in lifeboat 14, before she herself was pulled into the same boat. Harvey went down with the ship, with all their life savings in his inside pocket. Lottie re-married in 1914, and only two years later she succumbed to the tuberculosis which had plagued her for many years. A commemorative plaque for Harvey was placed on their former home.

Just before the lifeboat was lowered, Assistant Surgeon John Simpson handed a torch light to Fifth Officer Lowe, remarking 'Here is something that may be useful to you.'

The lifeboat's descent was stopped at A Deck and the crew shouted out if there were any women and children in the area, but there was no reply. As the descent continued, Fifth Officer Lowe was forced to have to fire two bullets down the side of the ship, which splashed into the water below, in an effort to warn any more individuals from trying to get in.

Then there was another problem. Able Seaman Scarrott recalled: 'The aft fall got twisted and we dropped the boat by releasing gear and when the boat was in the water we rowed clear of the ship.' Apparently, the problem caused a leak and water started pouring into the lifeboat.

He continued:

> The sight of that grand ship going down will never be forgotten. She slowly went down bow first with a slight list to starboard until the water reached the bridge then she went quicker. When the third funnel had nearly disappeared, I heard four explosions, which I took to be the bursting of the boilers. The ship was right up on end then. Suddenly she broke in two between the third and fourth funnel. The after part of the ship came down on the water in its normal position and seemed as if it was going to remain afloat, but it only remained a minute or two and then sank. The lights were burning right up until she broke in two. The cries from the poor souls struggling in the water seemed terrible in the stillness of the night. It seemed to go through you like a knife.

About 150 yards from where *Titanic* sank, they came upon lifeboats 4, 10, 12 and collapsible D. They were all filled with women and children, but there was no officer in charge of them. Fifth Officer Lowe wanted to go back to the wreck site to see if he could save any people from the water, so he decided to take charge and strung them all together. He thought that they would make a larger object to be seen from a passing ship.

He distributed his passengers among the other three lifeboats, and as the woman and children were being transferred, he was unimpressed to find that there was a man in the boat disguised as a woman, so he 'pitched' him into the other lifeboat. Able Seamen Frank Evans and Edward Buly were transferred from lifeboat 10 into lifeboat 14, as well as second-class passenger Charles Williams.

London-born Mr Williams was a married man and a successful racquets player, the sport which he coached at Harrow School. He had been playing in the squash court and was resting in the smoking room when the collision occurred. He estimated that the iceberg rose a hundred feet above the deck. It was originally reported that he had been lost in the sinking.

Able Seaman Scarrott suggested that more than one boat went back to the site of the sinking:

> Our officer (Lowe) then ordered all the boats under his charge to row towards where the ship went down to see if we could pick up anybody. Some of our boats picked up a few. I cannot say how many. After that we tied all our boats together so as to form a large object on the water which would be seen quicker than a single boat by a passing vessel. We divided the passengers of our boat amongst the other four, and then taking one man from each boat so as to make a crew we rode away amongst the wreckage as we heard cries for help coming from that direction.

Tom Threlfall was in lifeboat 14 and recalled:

> Then he [Fifth Officer Lowe] called to several other boats close by, 'Throw out your painters,' and we linked them all up. Mr Lowe passed about fifty women and children from his boat, and said, 'We will go for the wreckage,' to which other people were clinging. From the wreckage we picked up four men. Then Mr Lowe called out, 'There's a boat over there and she's sinking.' Although we were then towing a collapsible boat with about eighty people in her we reached the sinking boat just as the water was up to her gunwale and took twenty-six men and one woman, a Mrs Abbott, off her. I held the woman in my arms till we reached *Carpathia*.

Clear Cameron noted: 'Officer Lowe decided to go back to search for survivors and transferred all the passengers from lifeboat 14 into lifeboat 10. According to Nellie a 'madman' kept shaking the boat and they feared it would capsize, so he was pushed overboard. Lifeboat 14 was reportedly the only one which went back to look for survivors and six victims were pulled from the water, but two of them died.'

After Fifth Officer Lowe had allowed Charles Williams into the boat to help to row, some people expressed a fear that they might be swamped by desperate people if they returned, so he reluctantly agreed to wait until the screams from those in peril had died down a bit before he went back to help the desperate survivors. Lifeboat 14 made the journey of approximately 150 yards back to the disaster site, and when they arrived at the wreckage they were confronted with the dreadful sight of countless dead bodies floating in the icy water.

Joe Scarrott remembered:

> When we got to it the sight we saw was awful. We were amongst hundreds of dead bodies floating in lifebelts. We could only see four alive. The first one we picked up was a male passenger. He died shortly

> after we got him in the boat. After a hard struggle we managed to get the other three. One of these we saw kneeling as if in prayer upon what appeared to be a part of a staircase. He was only about 20 yards away from us but it took us half-an-hour to push our boat through the wreckage and bodies to get to him; even then we could not get very close, so we put out an oar for him to get hold of and so pulled him to the boat. All the bodies we saw seemed as if they had perished with the cold as their limbs were all cramped up. As we left that awful scene, we gave way to tears. It was enough to break the stoutest heart.

Ida Minahan did not speak favourably of Fifth Officer Lowe. She testified that at first he did not want to go back and was persuaded to do so by some of the women in the boat. She also alleged that he swore at her and said she suspected he had been drinking. However, her testimony is not supported by any of the other passengers, and it seems that she was mistaken about his decision to go back. It is understandable that the officer would have little patience with any of the passengers who were being awkward or inconsiderate, of which there were some, and he may well have sworn in the heat of the moment. As Ellen Walcroft stated: 'Officer Lowe wanted to go back to the rescue, but the women begged him not to go.' Lily Futrelle was of the opinion that Officer Lowe was, 'A leader with a cool head, desperate courage, and knowledge of the sea, who rescued people with his own hands.'

When they reached the area of the sinking, they did not find very many people still alive. First-class passenger William Hoyt was hauled on board, but died later. They had to push their way through many bodies to get to a steward named Harold Phillimore who was found clinging to the top of some wreckage that looked like a piece of staircase. They also found 17-year-old Fang Lang (Win Sun Fong), one of eight Chinese passengers, hanging on to a door. Some reported that there was a fourth man saved, but they have never been positively identified. Later they came across collapsible lifeboat A, which had several people on board and was filled with water. These poor people were taken off the stricken vessel into lifeboat 14. However, the story of collapsible lifeboat A was not yet over.

After rescuing all the survivors they could find in the water, Fifth Officer Lowe constructed a makeshift sail which allowed them to make more progress. As they did so, they saw collapsible D and sailed towards it. A rope was thrown to the vessel and it was taken in tow.

During the Board of Trade inquiry, Sir Robert Finlay summed up with the words:

> [Officer Lowe] waited, an operation of the most painful character, requiring great nerve and great coolness, he waited until the sea had done its work with the great majority of people, and then put back and picked up a few of the survivors. But to suggest, as some questions which were put suggested, that there was inhumanity in not pushing into the crowd of drowning people in the hope of saving them, is, I submit, a course based upon ignorance of the fundamental conditions that attend on the endeavour to save people who are struggling in the water when, if you push your boat among them, the only result will be that those in the boat are added to the roll of victims.

Joe Scarrott expressed his relief when he realised that they were going to be rescued:

> Just then we sighted the lights of a steamer, which proved to be the steamship *Carpathia* of the Cunard Line. What a relief that was. We then made sail and went back to our other boats. By this time day was just beginning to dawn.
>
> All our boats proceeded towards *Carpathia*. She had stopped right over where our ship had gone down. She had got our wireless message for assistance. When we got alongside, we were got aboard as soon as possible. We found some survivors had already been picked up. Everything was in readiness for us – dry clothes, blankets, beds, hot coffee, spirits, etc., everything to comfort us.
>
> I must say that the passengers when they were in the boats, especially the women, were brave and assisted the handling of the boats a great deal. Thank God the weather was fine, or I do not think there would have been one soul left to tell the tale. The last of the survivors were got aboard about 8:30am. The dead bodies that were in some of the boats were taken aboard and after identification were given a proper burial.
>
> We steamed about in the vicinity for a few hours in the hope of finding some more survivors, but we did not find any. During that time wives were enquiring for husbands, sisters for brothers, and children for their parents, but many a sad face told the result.
>
> *Carpathia* was bound from New York to Gibraltar, but the captain decided to return to New York with us. We arrived there about 9pm on Thursday the 18th. We had good weather during the trip, but it was a sad journey. A list of the survivors was taken as soon as we had left the scene of the disaster.
>
> On arrival at New York everything possible was ready for our immediate assistance – clothing, money, medical aid and good accommodation. In fact, I think it would have been impossible for the people of America to have treated us better.

LIFEBOAT 10

Lifeboat 10 was launched by Chief Officer Wilde and First Officer Murdoch at 1:50am from the portside at the rear of the ship. It was the last regular lifeboat to be launched, and Sailor John Poingdestre was placed in charge.

Chief Baker Joughin had got his staff of thirteen bakers together in the baker's shop on D Deck, and had each of them carry four loaves of bread up to the boat deck to be placed in the lifeboats. By this time things were looking desperate, and yet Mr Joughin said that some of the women were still apprehensive about getting into a lifeboat, and they actually ran away and down the steps to A Deck. Joughlin ran after them and had to force them back up to the boat deck, 'and practically threw them in.'

Able Seaman Frank Evans stated: 'It was necessary for the women and children on the sinking vessel to jump 3 feet from the deck to the lifeboats. Babies were tossed into the boats. This jump had to be made 70 feet above the sea, and the height was so terrifying that some of the women refused to attempt it, and several were thrown bodily across the gap.'

Third-class passengers Thomas and Elizabeth Davison were from Wiltshire and were on their way to settle in Ohio, where Elizabeth's parents lived. Tom was a blacksmith. It seems that they had not been disturbed from their sleep by the collision and it was very late when they got to the boat deck. There they saw 'men and women fighting about the lifeboats' and everyone was 'shouting and pushing about the boat.' Eventually, Elizabeth was grabbed and thrown into lifeboat 10, leaving Tom to a terrible fate. As they reached the sea, a man was seen to fall into the water from above them. There were thirty-five in the boat and some of them had to stand up, which caused it to list and take on water. 'The cold was intense and the women were only scantily clad.'

Mark Fortune, his wife Mary, three of their four daughters – Ethel Flora, Alice Elizabeth and Mabel – and one of their two sons – Charles

Alexander – had been on a tour of Europe, during which time Alice had gained an admirer in William Thomson Sloper, 'because she was a pretty girl and an excellent dancing partner.' While in Cairo earlier in the year, she had been approached by a fortune teller, who warned, 'You are in danger every time you travel on the sea, for I see you adrift in an open boat. You will lose everything but your life.'

Bertha Mulvihill was on her way back to the United States after attending her sister's wedding in Ireland. She had decided to surprise her fiancé, who was not aware that she was on her way home to him. She was accompanied by fellow Westmeath natives Eugene and Margaret Daly, and shared a third-class cabin with Margaret near one of the ship's boiler rooms.

After the collision they had to struggle through the chaos up to the boat deck, where all three of them jumped into lifeboat 10, which Bertha likened to jumping off the roof of a three-storey building, even breaking three ribs in the fall. Eugene was ordered to get back out of the boat, but he refused, until gunfire rang out and he got back onto the deck. Bertha remembered, 'Dawn was just breaking when I saw a light way off in the distance. Then two big green lights broke through the mist. We cheered and cheered. Some cried. I just sat and offered up a little prayer.' Eugene eventually left the ship on the collapsible B.

Joseph and Juliette Laroche, with their daughters, 1-year-old Louise and 3-year-old Simone, joined *Titanic* at Cherbourg as second-class passengers. Joseph was one of the few Black men on board and was the only Haitian person, being a direct descendant of the father of Haitian independence and related to two Haitian presidents. As an engineer, he had been involved in the construction of the Parisian railway. His two girls had been born in Paris and his French wife Juliette was pregnant with their third child.

Louise suffered medical problems, and racial discrimination in France prevented Joseph from getting a well-paid job. As they needed more money to pay for Louise's high medical bills, Joseph decided to take his family back to his native Haiti to try to find a better-paying engineering job. However, after leading his family to lifeboat 10, Joseph was not allowed to board with them, and he lost his life in the sinking. Juliette gave birth to their son, Joseph Junior, towards the end of the year.

Masabumi Hosono was the only Japanese passenger onboard *Titanic* and, being a man, he accepted that the women and children first policy had sealed his fate. However, when a crew member shouted that there were two spaces left in lifeboat 10, Hosono jumped in at the last moment. He was not well received by some of the female passengers, who had left their men behind, and some of them suggested that they should throw him overboard, but this was not carried out.

Elin Hakkarainen, from third class, may have been the woman who nearly fell into the sea:

> One of the officers pointed at me saying, 'Room for one more lady. Come on, hurry!' As I stepped into the boat, it was already moving downward. I lost my balanced [*sic*], almost falling between the lifeboat and ship until someone in the lifeboat grabbed my arm and pulled me into a seat. On the way down we stopped at a lower deck and picked up one more lady. Our lifeboat did not return to the spot where the *Titanic* went down. Our lifeboat reached the *Carpathia* at 7:30am. We were one of the last boats to be picked up. I finally located Anna Sjöblom, who had knocked on my cabin door to awaken me. We had become separated in the rush to the upper deck and had entered separate lifeboats.

The youngest survivor, Millvina Dean, was in lifeboat 10, together with her mother and brother. Her brother was taken care of by Florence Thorneycroft, who was with them. There were perhaps seven or eight ladies from first class, possibly fifteen or more second-class passengers, and possibly ten or twelve third-class passengers, apart from the four crew, in the boat: a total of perhaps forty people.

After reaching the water, they moved a safe distance from the ship before joining a flotilla consisting of lifeboats 4, 12, 14 and collapsible D. Fifth Officer Lowe, in charge of lifeboat 14, ordered that Edward Buley and Frank Evans leave lifeboat 10 and help to row lifeboat 14 as it returned to the scene of the sinking to try to rescue survivors from the water. At the same time, several people transferred into lifeboat 10 from lifeboat 14.

William Burke, from lifeboat 10, later testified that after they had drifted about practically all night, he had ordered that his lifeboat be cut adrift, after they had become aware of the upside-down lifeboat B needing assistance. Lifeboats 4 and 12 then went to the assistance of lifeboat B. He said that they then drifted. He also mentioned that by the time they had arrived at *Carpathia,* they had been tied to another lifeboat, possibly lifeboat 12.

COLLAPSIBLES

LIFEBOAT A

At 2:10am, after collapsible C had been launched on the starboard side of the ship, Chief Officer Wilde, First Officer Murdoch and Sixth Officer Moody attempted to attach lifeboat A to the same davit. Unfortunately, time had run out, as the ship was going down fast. The sea water had begun to engulf the deck and the lifeboat was washed over the side before the canvas sides had been put up. It became awash with water after the supports for its canvas sides were broken from the fall. Air tanks built into the craft prevented it from sinking entirely, and as their last desperate chance, several people climbed on to it, but their weight turned it over and they were thrown back into the water. However, some did manage to climb back on board.

Officers Murdoch, Wilde and Moody were lost at about this time. They were either swept away and drowned or possibly hit by *Titanic's* funnel as it crashed into the water. Second Officer Lightoller stated that he saw First Officer Murdoch being dragged away by a wave; Colonel Gracie wrote that he witnessed Chief Officer Wilde being washed away; and a lamp trimmer named Samuel Ernest Hemming reported that he saw Sixth Officer Moody being washed off the deck, before he too was washed off, but he managed to reach lifeboat 4 and scramble aboard.

Richard 'Dick' Williams had made a name for himself as a promising lawn tennis player and was travelling back to America with his father Charles, who was a direct descendant of Benjamin Franklin, to play in tournaments and to enrol at Harvard. They had intended to return earlier on a different ship, but Dick had suffered from a bout of measles and they had had to delay their journey.

They had left their first-class stateroom on C Deck intending to go to the bar for drinks, and on the way had come across a steward who was trying to open a stuck door, which had passengers panicking in the room on the other side. In an attempt to help the situation, Richard rammed his shoulder against the door and broke in. The occupants were thankful, but the steward huffily warned him that he would report him to the White Star Line for damaging their property. To top it all, when they got to the bar, another steward told them that it was closed, so they went to the gymnasium instead.

When they realised that the situation was serious, they went up to the boat deck, where they found that only the collapsible boats were left, and they had to dive for their lives. Unfortunately, when the funnel collapsed and crashed into the sea, Dick lost sight of his father. He stated: 'I was not underwater very long, and as soon as I came to the top I threw off my big fur coat. About 20 yards away I saw something floating. I swam to it and found it to be a collapsible boat [A].' He also took off his shoes, which may have been a bad mistake as the bone-chilling water posed a serious threat to his limbs.

There may have been about thirty people balancing or clinging to the flat boat as it drifted away from the disaster area, all shivering with cold and up to their knees in cold water, and one by one they succumbed to the stress and cold. After awful suffering while floating precariously for several hours, Dick and about ten other survivors were eventually transferred to lifeboat D, which was then attached to lifeboat 14 and towed to *Carpathia*. The collapsible A craft was abandoned and left floating on the water.

When he was taken on board the rescue ship, the doctor examined his leg and fearing hypothermia and gangrene, advised amputation. However, Dick refused, 'I am going to need these legs,' he insisted. As he tried to stand up, he remembered, 'It was like thousands of needles.' However, determined to restore feelings in his legs, he walked the deck of the ship at regular intervals. A few months later he was back playing tennis, going on to win the United States Championships in 1914 and 1916, the latter as the world number one player, and becoming an Olympic gold medallist in 1924.

Rhoda, Rossmore and Eugene Abbott had been asleep when a steward alerted them, and they put on lifejackets and went up to the second-class saloon area. Rossmore is said to have dropped to his knees and prayed that his mother might be saved even if he and his brother were not. All three were allowed to approach the emergency lifeboat C, but when Rhoda realised that her sons were not being allowed to board the craft with her, she stepped back.

As the ship sank and the sea engulfed the deck, they were all swept overboard. Rhoda tried to clasp hold of her sons but to no avail. She swam around in the freezing water for some time trying to find them, but then saw collapsible A and struggled to get on board. Rhoda is believed to have been the only woman who went in the water and survived. Her legs were badly injured, but she was glad she remained on *Titanic* until the last because it allowed her to remain with her sons. Rossmore's body was recovered, but Eugene's was not.

Whilst on a west-bound voyage, the White Star liner RMS *Oceanic* found the 'collapsible A' lifeboat on 13 May adrift on the ocean, about 190 miles from the disaster area. It contained the decomposed bodies of a Canadian businessman, a first-class passenger named Thomson Beattie, still wearing his dinner suit, and two firemen, whose hair had been bleached by the sun and salt. The bodies were in such a bad state that their limbs detached from their bodies when the crew tried to move them. All three bodies were placed in plastic bags, draped in Union Jacks, and put into the sea. Thomas Beattie's body was buried on his mother's birthday, in the area of the sea where she had been born on a ship bound for Canada. They also found an inscribed ring, believed to have belonged to a Swedish couple who had died during the evacuation.

Several newspapers reported the find: 'The body of a fireman has been found in a boat by the *Oceanic* chained by the leg to the thwart, and the bodies of two men were huddled together and had corks in their mouths. The *Oceanic*'s doctor believes the men chewed them in their delirium to ease the pangs of hunger and thirst.'

The craft was hauled onto *Oceanic's* deck and taken to New York. There it joined the other thirteen recovered lifeboats in a loft assigned to the White Star Line between piers 59 and 60. They are known to have remained in the loft throughout the December of 1912, during which time they were twice surveyed for insurance purposes. Their final disposition is unknown, but it is believed that they may have been transferred to RMS *Olympic* and possibly other White Star liners.

LIFEBOAT B

By this time the water had risen almost as high as the boat deck, as Second Officer Lightoller climbed on to the top of the officers' quarters, stripped the covers off lifeboat B and cut away the ropes with a penknife. He was able to send the craft down to the flooded deck, but it flipped over, and the assistant Marconi operator Harold Bride became trapped under it. *Titanic* took a great plunge forward, so Second Officer Lightoller turned to face the sea and dived off the deck. When he surfaced, he started to swim clear, but he was sucked against the grating of one of the large ventilator shafts and was taken down with the ship as it slipped under the surface. As the water hit the still hot boilers, the blast blew him back to the surface, where he found himself alongside the capsized collapsible B, to which he and Harold Bride grabbed on. As *Titanic* went down, the rear funnel broke loose and toppled his way, narrowly missing him as it crashed into the water.

Jack Phillips was so busy with his work in the Marconi room that Harold Bride had to put on his lifebelt for him, and then he went back to their rooms to collect some belongings. As he was doing so, he happened to look out of the door and saw a big man from 'below decks' leaning over Jack and sneakily trying to slip the lifejacket off his back. Knowing how gallantly his colleague was behaving, Harold became angry at what the selfish man was doing, so he picked something up and hit him with it. The man was knocked senseless, and they left him lying motionless on the wireless room floor.

After the collision, Colonel Gracie met Fred Wright, the squash court attendant, who looked quite worried. Probably to reassure the 24-year-old a bit, the colonel said jokingly, 'Hadn't we better cancel that appointment?' The reason for Mr Wright's worried look was because he knew that the squash court and his cabin were flooded, but he simply replied, 'Yes, we better.' Fred Wright could not swim and lost his life in the sinking; as did Thomas McCawley, who looked after the gymnasium.

Colonel Gracie stated that he was driven to the topmost deck and saw no other survivor. After the waves swept the liner, he grasped the railings desperately but was forced to release his hold when the ship plunged. He swirled round for what seemed an interminable time and eventually came to the surface. He seized a wooden grating and by the time he recovered his breath, he discovered a large canvas and cork raft. He and another struggled to the collapsible B boat.

Not long after his rescue, Colonel Gracie wrote a book entitled *The Truth about the Titanic,* and soon after that passed away, probably due in part to the trauma of that night on the doomed ship.

Southampton-born Walter 'Wally' Hurst, who had made the remark concerning the lack of people in emergency lifeboat B, remained on deck until near the end. His father-in-law, William Mintram, who had a history of violence, was also a fireman on the ship. They met each other just before *Titanic* went down. William had a lifejacket and gave it to Wally. It was an act of courage which probably saved his son-in-law's life at the cost of his own.

Wally stated:

> Well, I saw the forward part of the boat deck dip underwater so I jumped overboard, swam away from the ship, and turned around to look at her, but down came the funnel and smashed into the water right in front of my face. I got a gush of wind and dirt through that nearly blinded me, and I felt the cap go off my head and one slipper off my foot.
>
> But I didn't take my attention off this boat that I see – the collapsible boat washed straight over off the deck within a few yards of me. But I managed to get on it, and I was followed quickly by the second officer and a few others. Anyhow, she soon got filled up.
>
> There was an old man next to me and he was complaining all night long that his head was cold. Well, I took particular to that because mine was pretty cold too. But a friend of mine, a shipmate named Lindsay gave me a drink from a bottle. I thought I was on a good thing, I think it was whisky or brandy. Instead of that, it was essence of peppermint. It nearly choked me!

Fireman Charles William Lindsay was a Bristolian who had served in the Boer War of 1899–1902 as a driver with the rank of lance corporal in the Royal Engineers.

Algernon Barkworth stated: 'Coming over I made the acquaintance of two most agreeable chaps.' They were Arthur Gee and Charles Jones, and he was with them in the first-class smoking room,

'...discussing with them late on Sunday night the science of good road building in which I am keenly interested.

I was sitting in the smoking room with my friends when we heard a grinding sound which caused the ship to tremble and the engines seemed to stop. Walking out on deck, through the smoking rooms veranda of deck A, the first person I saw was Mr T Stead and I asked him what he had seen. He said, 'an iceberg had ground against the starboard side.' I went forward and noticed the forecastle filled with pieces of ice which had fallen from the friction of the ship against the iceberg. The forecastle made a heavy list to the starboard.

I noticed that the band was playing a waltz tune. Soon afterwards we went to see the boats lowered. The escaping steam making a deafening sound, women and children were put into the boats first. When most of the boats had left the ship, she began to list forward.

Jones and Gee were looking over the side. I learned swimming at Eton and made up my mind if it came to the worst I would try my luck in the water. When the ship gave the first dip, we all went aft. Well, I had read somewhere that a ship which is about to sink gives a premonitory dip, and when the Titanic did that, I simply chucked my despatch case, containing all my money and some papers, into the scuppers, Jones and Gee were standing by, with arms on the rail, looking down. I imagine they were preparing for death.

Algernon was able to put his swimming skills to good use:

I had on a fur coat with the lifebelt strapped to the outside... [Stating later that it made him look like 'some waterlogged sheepdog']. When I came up, I swam for all I was worth to get away from the sinking ship.

Coming across a floating plank, I rested upon it. Looking over my shoulder I saw the *Titanic* disappear with a volley of loud reports, so I swam slowly around and came luckily upon an overturned lifeboat [collapsible B]. I climbed upon this at this time. The screams of the drowning was most terrible. Several more people climbed up the stern of the boat, which was now full. We competed to keep everyone else from gathering upon it.

We drifted until daybreak when we sighted the *Carpathia* about 5 miles off. Shortly after that we got near to the *Titanic* lifeboat, which rescued us from our perilous position. With daylight, a strong breeze arose which threatened to submerge us. When we were rescued the water was up to our knees. We had two dead men on our stern, one of which fell off. The other one was taken aboard *Carpathia* and was afterwards buried [at sea]. When taken aboard we were treated most kindly.

Edward Arthur Dorkings was the 18-year-old son of a policeman, who, it was said, was being sent to stay with his uncle and aunt in Chicago because he was 'openly gay'. He was almost refused permission to board *Titanic* because a doctor noticed his bloodshot eyes, but he gave the reason that he had travelled overnight to Southampton, and it was caused by lack of sleep and not by any kind of illness.

Edward was in the music room playing cards with some of his fellow travellers when the shock of the collision threw them off the bench on which they had been sitting. He said that he saw a large iceberg as he went on deck to investigate, and on seeing that the ship was in peril, he took off his shoes and outer garments and plunged down into the cold water.

As he was swimming about in the water struggling to stay at the surface, collapsible B came floating past and he grabbed hold of a part of it. Two men who had lost their grip on the boat clung to his legs for a short while before they let loose and floated away. Eventually, several hands pulled him on board. He passed out from the cold and came to just as *Carpathia* appeared in the distance.

Lifeboat 10 was Chief Baker Joughin's assigned vessel, but he did not get on board. He went down to A Deck, from where he threw about fifty deck chairs into the sea, which he hoped would act as flotation devises. Then he went to the deck pantry to get a drink of water, where he heard a loud crash, 'as part of the ship had buckled.' Knowing that he had little time left, he ran to the starboard side of the poop deck, climbed over the safety rail, and as the ship went down, he remained where he was and rode it down like an elevator, keeping his head above the water until he dived off. It seems that he was the last survivor to leave *Titanic* before she went down.

Joughin kept paddling and treading water in the near-freezing ocean for around two hours before he spied the upturned emergency B. He swam towards it, but there was no room. Fortunately, one of his fellow bakers, Isaac Maynard was balancing on the craft, and on seeing him he grabbed his hand as Joughlin held on to the side of the boat. Lifeboat 12 then appeared and he swam over to it and was taken aboard. Despite his dreadful ordeal, he was rescued by *Carpathia* with only swollen feet.

Like his boss, Isaac Maynard had remained on the deck until *Titanic* went down, and he stated: 'I saw Captain Smith washed from the Bridge and afterwards saw him swimming in the water. He was still fully dressed, with his peak cap on his head. One of the men clinging to the raft tried to save him by reaching out a hand, but he would not let him, and called out, "Look after yourselves, boys!" I do not know what became of the captain, for I could not see him at the time, but I suppose he sank.'

Second Officer Lightoller took charge of the thirty men on the upturned collapsible B, and Harold Bride estimated it would take *Carpathia* 'an hour or so' to get to them. Regular lifeboats 4, 10 and 12 eventually began to separate from Lowe's craft, and at about 4:30am, as daylight began to appear, Second Officer Lightoller saw lifeboats 4 and 12 drifting around in the distance, so he took out a whistle and used it to gain the attention of the people in the other two boats, calling for them to row over to him. He and some of the men from the upturned boat got into lifeboat 12 and the rest got into lifeboat 4, while collapsible B was left drifting in the water.

While Salon Steward Tom Whiteley was assisting to launch the lifeboats, he was caught by a rope as it was being uncoiled and thrown into the sea. His lifebelt kept him afloat until he found an oak wardrobe that rose to the surface after the *Titanic* sank. At daybreak he saw a collapsible raft black with men, all standing. He swam to it but was not allowed on board. He was told, 'it's thirty lives against yours.' He prayed that someone on the raft might die so that he might take his place. Someone did die shortly afterwards, and he was then allowed on board.

Jack Thayer was aged 17 when he boarded *Titanic* at Cherbourg with his parents, Marian and John and Marian's maid Margaret Fleming. After the collision Jack Thayer went on deck to investigate both at the front and the back of the vessel. He woke his parents, who accompanied him back on deck, and when they realised the ship was beginning to list, they went back to their cabins and put on warmer clothes and lifejackets. They returned to the deck, but Jack became separated from his parents. After a while he came across a man named Milton Long, whom he had met a few hours previously. As he was a good swimmer, Jack proposed that they should jump off the ship, but after looking how far the drop was down to the water, Mr Long went against the idea.

However, when the ship lunged forward dramatically, they agreed to attempt the task. Long jumped backwards with his face towards the ship, and he perished. Jack launched himself over the rail, and on reaching the water, he began to swim for his life, eventually reaching collapsible B. After balancing precariously on the upturned raft, he was rescued into lifeboat 12. While he was on board *Carpathia*, he described to an American named Lewis Skidmore how he saw *Titanic* as she sank and he drew sketches based on his description.

Collapsible B was recovered by the CS *Mackay-Bennett*.

LIFEBOAT C

Collapsible lifeboat C was launched from the starboard side at 2am by Chief Officer Wilde and First Officer Murdoch, with some assistance from Purser McElroy. They took the craft from its storage, lifted the sides, and fitted it to the davits that they had used to launch emergency lifeboat 1 about forty-five minutes earlier.

Quartermasters Rowe and Arthur Bright were attempting to send makeshift Morse code signals by using a bright light on *Titanic,* hoping to attract any ships that may have been in the vicinity to the north. Captain Smith was observing the events from the starboard side of the Bridge, from where he told them to stop what they were doing and instead go and help launch collapsible C. About forty people were in the craft when Officer Wilde called out for any more women and children, but there was no reply.

A group of stewards and third-class passengers decided to rush the boat and climb aboard. Purser McElroy drove most of them back, but two did manage to get in.

Quartermaster Rowe remembered seeing two men get in at the back of the boat before it was lowered. One of them is believed to have been Bruce Ismay, whose decision to save himself became controversial.

The other may have been 34-year-old Joseph Hyman, known as Abe to his family, who was described as a framer when he boarded *Titanic* as a third-class passenger. He was going to America to join his brother in Virginia, with the aim of setting up a new life there, and his wife and five children were going to join him from Manchester once he was established.

Joseph had gone to his room at a fairly early hour and was sleeping soundly when at about 11:43pm he was awakened by a slight jar. He did not think it was sufficient to cause any alarm, but when the engines stopped, he got dressed and went on deck to see what the trouble was. As he went down the corridor from the bow end of the boat to the stern on his way to the ladder, leading from the steerage to the topmost deck, he was reassured as he passed a number of stokers, engineers, fireman, and stewards, all laughing, just as if nothing serious had occurred.

He climbed the ladder to the top deck, where he saw a few people standing around and spoke with several of them. They all felt that the *Titanic* was too perfect a ship to be wrecked. He could not remember a more beautiful night. Stars were shining brightly, and the heavens were clearer than he had ever seen them before. Everything was quiet.

His first thought of danger came when signal rockets were fired from the topmost deck, even though he thought that this was done simply to warn some passing vessel that the boat had been disabled. However, no sooner had the signal rockets been fired when orders were given to lower the boats.

The Lebanese family of Hinnah Tu'mah (Hannah Thomas) and her young children Mariyam and Jirjis, were on their way to Michigan to be with her husband Darwīsh, who had been working there as an onion farmer since 1905. Their journey began when they left their village with others by camel caravan to Beirut on the eastern coast of the Mediterranean Sea and journeyed by freighter to Marseille and from there to Cherbourg, where they boarded *Titanic* as third-class passengers. There were many other Lebanese nationals on the ship and the two children spent their time running around the stairwells and passages, and playing in spare cabins.

On the night of the sinking, Hinnah put Jirjis to bed and began to get worried because Mariyam had not returned from playing out. She was standing at the door to the cabin anxiously waiting for her when the crash happened. Hinnah took Jirjis in her arms and went up to the boat deck to ask what had happened, telling the little boy to stay where she had put him while she went back to look for her daughter. When she got back to the cabin, she was relieved to find Mariyam, who had fallen asleep in one of the spare cabins. They went back up to the boat deck, where they found Jiris looking very anxious because several people had tried to coax him to get into a lifeboat without her. They all got into a lifeboat, believed to be collapsible C.

Nicholas Nasrallah had moved from Lebanon to San Francisco to be with other members of his family. However, aged 29 in early 1912, he had returned to his home country to look for a suitable wife and had found one in 17-year-old Adal 'Adele' Hakim. By the time they boarded *Titanic* at Cherbourg, Adele was already pregnant. On the night of the disaster Nicholas escorted Adele to a lifeboat, where he said goodbye and did not attempt to enter. He lost his life, and his body was later recovered by the *Mackay-Bennett*. Mrs Nasrallah put in a claim for £10,000 for the loss of her husband and £2,000 for that of her baggage and jewellery. She gave birth to a son she called Nicholas later in the year, but he only survived for a few hours.

After the collision, Frank and Emily Goldsmith, their son Frankie, along with Thomas Theobald and Alfred Rush, made their way up to the starboard side of the boat deck. When Emily and Frankie were led into the collapsible C craft, Frank stood back and bid them goodbye. Tom Theobald realised the gravity of the situation and gave Emily his wedding ring to give to his wife Mary, who, it seemed, had already travelled to Detroit. Emily stated later: 'Frank and Alfred were close to the rail on the deck below as we were lowered past it, but we were all so dazed that we hardly said a word, just waved our hands. I thought then they would be able to get away on another boat or raft.'

Fang Lang (Win Sun Fong), the youngest of the eight Chinese men on board *Titanic,* had been picked up out of the water by Fifth Officer Lowe in lifeboat 14, while two other Chinese men named Len Lam and Lee Ling were drowned. That left five others, who are thought to have been in collapsible lifeboat C. They were Lee Bing, the only married man; Chang Chip; Choong Foo; and Ah Lam, all in their thirties, and 24-year-old Ling Hee.

They were all seamen who had boarded *Titanic* at Southampton on the same third-class ticket. They were out of work due to the coal strike and were on their way to join the Donald Lines freighter *Anetta,* which was docked at New York and was chartered by the Atlantic Fruit Company to sail to Cuba. Within twenty-four hours they were expelled from the United States because of the Chinese Exclusion Act, and the story of their plight was told in a successful 2021 film called *The Six.*

The Western Star and Roma Advertiser (Queensland) for 24 April 1912, reported:

> Mr Ismay has emphatically declared that he was simply a passenger on *Titanic,* that he was neither consulted regarding the speed at which the vessel travelled nor its navigation. He had not made any suggestions on these matters, and that he only saw the captain occasionally, and then never in his room or on the bridge, until after the collision with the iceberg. Mr Ismay declared that it was false to say that he desired the *Titanic* to make a record, and he continued, 'When I entered a boat with a passenger named Carter not a woman or other passenger remained on deck.' Mr Ismay added that the disaster had proved the futility of imagining that unsinkable vessels can be built.
>
> William Carter, the passenger referred to by Mr Ismay, has been interviewed at Philadelphia. He emphasised the injustice with 'which Mr Ismay is being treated.' He said, 'Ismay and I and several officers

walked up and down the deck of the sinking vessel for several minutes shouting, "Any more women?" There was no response, and the officers then said that Ismay and I could enter the boat if we would consent to row. This we did until the *Carpathia* was sighted.'

Mr Carter arrived at the rescue ship before the rest of his family and waited on deck for lifeboat 4 to appear. He remembered that he did not recognise his son under the big lady's hat and called out for him. Apparently, in response to second steward George Dodd's order that no more boys were to enter lifeboat 4, his mother had put the hat on his head, stating that as he looked like a girl he should be allowed on the lifeboat – which he was. Mr Carter is reported to have been 'much shaken by his experience and his face showed lines of suffering.'

LIFEBOAT D

Collapsible D was launched from the portside at about 2:05am, from the same davits that had been used to launch emergency lifeboat 2, with Chief Officer Wilde and Second Officer Lightoller taking charge of the procedure. As collapsible lifeboats A and B were washed off the boat deck soon after collapsible D, it was the last craft to be actually launched. The ship's list to the portside had caused a gap to appear between the boat deck and the lifeboat, which left the passengers with the daunting task of having to jump across the gap, and any slip could send them crashing down into the freezing cold water, which was by now only about 10 feet from the deck.

While the lifeboat was being loaded, Chief Officer Wilde asked Second Officer Lightoller to board and stay with it to take charge, but he refused, so Quartermaster Arthur Bright, who had assisted in firing the rockets, was put in charge. Second Officer Lightoller ordered a locked-arm circle of crew members around collapsible D so that only women and children could get through.

Henry Harris was a theatre manager and the owner of several prominent New York establishments. He had met with great success as the producer of *The Lion and the Mouse* in 1905. Among several well-known theatrical people of the time, he helped with the careers of Lillie Langtry and Mae West. He was travelling in cabin C83 with his wife Irene, known as Renee. A business acquaintance named John Baumann was with them. After Renee was placed in collapsible D, Henry and John stepped back and lost their lives in the sinking. The largest claim for losses concerning the *Titanic* disaster was £200,000, put forward by Renee. Among her losses was a pearl necklace valued at £2,000.

First-class passenger Hugh Woolner, the son of a member of the Royal Academy, had gained a blue at Cambridge for the hammer throw, and was described as 'a man of tremendous physical strength, standing 6 feet 3 inches tall and muscled like a Hercules', and went on to become a successful London stockbroker. Occupying cabin C52, at the time of the collision he was having a drink in the café, talking to Maurice Stephenson. While walking up and down the deck, Mr Woolner had tried to persuade Mr and Mrs Straus to get into a lifeboat and remembered seeing what he described as 'A continent of ice'. He and Stephenson were standing on the promenade deck just below where collapsible lifeboat D was swinging on its davits. As the boat began to drop down the side of the ship, water began to flood the deck where they were standing, so they both jumped aboard as it reached them. Mr Stephenson landed upside down in a heap at the bow of the craft, while Mr Woolner did not quite make it fully into the lifeboat and had to be pulled the rest of the way by some of the occupants.

On learning that the ship was in distress, it is said that Michel Navratil and some other passengers dressed his boys as best they could and took them up to the boat deck; other sources say they had just blankets wrapped around them. On arriving at collapsible D, Michel handed the boys through Second Officer Lightoller's guard around the craft, stating to his elder son, 'My child, when your mother comes for you, as she surely will, tell her that I loved her dearly, and still do. Tell her I expected her to follow us, so that we might all live happily together in the peace and freedom of the New World.' Michel perished in the disaster, and his was body number fifteen picked up by the *Mackay-Bennett*. The two boys became known as 'The Titanic Orphans', and while they were on board *Carpathia* they played with Bebe, the dog belonging to Margaret Hays, who had escaped in lifeboat 7. Margaret could converse with them because she spoke French, and she took them under her wing. They were eventually returned to their mother.

Frederick Hoyt was an American broker and a noted member of the New York Yacht Club, who owned several prestigious yachts and took part in international races. He and his wife Jane boarded at Southampton and occupied first-class cabin C93. After being told it would be best for them to get up onto the boat deck, Mr Hoyt suggested they should get warmly clad. He also stated that he looked out from the ship and saw *Titanic*'s lights reflecting on a large iceberg.

Mr Hoyt escorted his wife to a lifeboat and saw her safely aboard, but just before the craft was lowered, Mrs Hoyt saw that her husband was still on the deck and she scrambled back out again. The next minute she was picked up by a member of the crew and forced into lifeboat D. After sharing a glass of water with Captain Smith, whom he had known for many years, Mr Hoyt watched collapsible D being lowered and rowed away from the side of the ship. As he considered himself to be a good swimmer, Mr Hoyt decided to dive overboard and swim in the direction he thought the boat would go. He did so, and after using a piece of wreckage as buoyancy, he found that his calculations were correct and was only person to be picked up by collapsible D, the last boat to be rowed away from the ship. Mrs Hoyt was not aware that her husband was in the boat until they reached *Carpathia*, which was at about 7:15am.

***

An at-a-glance list and approximate time schedule concerning the launching of the lifeboats:

Time	*place*	*number*	*launchers*
12:40	starboard for	lifeboat 7	Murdoch and Lowe
12:45	starboard for	lifeboat 5	Murdoch, Lowe and Pitman
12:55	starboard for	lifeboat 3	Murdoch and Lowe
(12: 55	portside for	lifeboat 4	Wilde and Lightoller - not successfully)
01:00	portside for	lifeboat 8	Wilde and Lightoller
01:05	starboard for	lifeboat E1	Murdoch and Lowe
01:10	portside for	lifeboat 6	Lightoller
01:20	portside aft	lifeboat 16	Wilde, Moody and Lightoller
01:25	portside aft	lifeboat 14	Wilde, Moody, Lightoller and Lowe
01:30	portside aft	lifeboat 12	Wilde and Lightoller
01:30	starboard aft	lifeboat 9	Murdoch and Moody
01:35	starboard aft	lifeboat11	Murdoch and Moody
01:40	starboard aft	lifeboat 13	Murdoch and Moody
01:40	starboard aft	lifeboat 15	Murdoch and Moody
01:45	portside for	lifeboat E2	Wilde and Boxhall
01:50	portside for	lifeboat 4	Lightoller
01:50	portside aft	lifeboat 10	Murdoch and Wilde
02:00	starboard	lifeboat CC	Murdoch and Wilde
02:05	portside	lifeboat CD	Wilde and Lightoller
02:10	starboard	lifeboat CA	Murdoch, Wilde and Moody
02:10	portside	lifeboat CB	Lightoller

for = forward (front)

aft = (rear)

E = emergency

The *Daily Telegraph's* New York correspondent reported on 17 January 1913 on 'Titanic Claims – Total of over £1,100,000':

> Amongst the claims in connection with the *Titanic* disaster filed here, some in respect of 'mental and physical suffering' by survivors and relations. The total amount asked is now over £1,100,000. No claims have been submitted by Mrs John Jacob Astor, by the Wideners of Philadelphia, or by the family of Mr Charles Hays, former president of the Grand Trunk Railroad. The brother of Major Archibald Butt, military attaché to President Taft, put in a claim for the loss of his brother's personal baggage, but asked nothing for the loss of the major's life.

'ASLEEP IN THE DEEP'

The title of this chapter is taken from the 'In Memoriam' columns in the *Manchester Evening News,* devoted to Steward George Barlow. It is dedicated to a selection of victims who did not survive the sinking. George was born on 3 May 1872, at 4 Eveson Street in the Greengate district of Salford (birth certificate: CQ109711). As many as ten people from that city were associated with the RMS *Titanic* disaster.

Thomas Andrews made a point of sailing with a team of engineers on the maiden voyages of many of his ships; and *Titanic* would be no different. Thus, he selected some men from the Harland & Wolff workforce to accompany *Titanic* on its maiden voyage. They were given the collective title 'The Guarantee Group'. All nine members of the Guarantee Group were lost in the sinking.

The Guarantee Group was only decided shortly before the maiden voyage. The prospect of a place on the Guarantee Group was a powerful incentive to work hard and make a good impression with the bosses. Being selected to the Guarantee Group represented Harland & Wolff's confidence in you as an employee and was a reward for doing a good job. Only the best employees would make the grade and make the voyage.

The team of young men were responsible with overseeing the smooth running of the vessel during its maiden voyage, and to troubleshoot any problems such as any unfinished work or find and fix any problems that might arise during the voyage. They were to gather information and recommend any improvements. They were treated as crew members and most of them occupied cabins in second class.

The Guarantee Group consisted of master shipbuilder Thomas Andrews (a married man, aged 39, resided in Belfast); chief draughtsman Roderick Robert Crispin Chisholm (a married man, aged 43, from Dumbarton); assistant manager of the electrical department William Henry Marsh Parr (a married man, aged 29, from Wigan); apprentice electrician Ennis Hastings Watson (aged 18, from Belfast); apprentice joiner William Campbell (aged 20, from Belfast); apprentice engine fitter Alfred Fleming Cunningham (aged 21, from Belfast); outside foreman engineer Anthony Wood Frost (a married man, aged 38, from Kingston-upon-Hull); leading hand engineer Robert Knight (a married man, aged 42, from Belfast); and apprentice plumber Frank Parkes (aged 21, from Belfast).

There should have been ten members of the Guarantee Group, but Liam Flaherty, a Catholic shipwright and joiner, forfeited his place because his father, a fellow ship-worker, was beaten up by some of the Protestant workers at Harland & Wolff and told not to return to his job. The attack saved Liam's life.

After *Titanic* collided with the iceberg, Mr Andrews inspected the damage and determined her chances of survival. Suspecting that she was doomed, he spoke with Captain Smith and gave him the grave news that he did not expect the ship to remain afloat for more than two hours. He and his small group went about urging evacuation and inspecting for open port lights to slow the rate of flooding. The electricians went to the engine spaces to help the men who were already there to keep the lights burning as long as possible.

***

As noted, two members of the Guarantee Group were electricians named William Parr and Ennis Watson. There were eight electricians in all, and they all lost their lives while trying to keep the lights on so that people could see their way to the lifeboats.

Among those who died was the chief electrician Peter Sloan, a married man from Liverpool, who received £12 a month in wages. He had been on board RMS *Baltic* when she came to the assistance of the White Star liner RMS *Republic* and the Italian ship SS *Florida*, which had collided with each other on 23 January 1909, causing the *Republic* to sink. He volunteered to take part in the rescue work, for which he received a silver medal from the Lloyds committee. He was also on board RMS *Olympic* when it crashed with HMS *Hawke*. He was a good sportsman, excelling at football and swimming.

The second electrician was Alf Allsop, who had been one of the transfer crew which brought *Titanic* to Southampton, where he signed-on, for which he would receive £11 a month. He came from a Manchester family of sixteen children and became well-known in the district, spending much of his time riding on the electric tram cars in Manchester. He was also a regular visitor at the Salford power station in Bloom Street. It is said that he crossed the Atlantic on RMS *Oceanic* about 100 times before joining *Titanic*. He developed an idea for a multi-clutched lifeboat winch powered by an electric motor, which he named 'The Allsop Electric Lifeboat Crane.'

The other four electricians who were doomed to die were the two Irish lads named Alfred Middleton and Albert Ervine, who were working on the funnel when *Titanic* left Southampton; Herbert Jupe of Southampton, who always took his ukulele with him on voyages; and William Kelly of Glasgow, a Roman Catholic who described in a letter how he endured some of the anti-Catholic sentiment shown in the Harland & Wolff shipyard at that time.

***

Thirty-four Swedish nationals survived the sinking of *Titanic*, but perhaps the most tragic incident concerning the disaster was that of the native-Swedish Skoog party, who all went down with the ship: Wilhelm Skoog, his wife Anna, and their four children Harold, Mabel, Margit and Karl, who had been involved in a railway accident during which his leg was severed meaning he had to use crutches to get around. The party also included Jenny Henriksson and Elin Nathalia Pettersson, who were believed to have been family cousins.

The Skoog family lived at Iron Mountain in Michigan, where Wilhelm was an engineer at the Pewabic Mine, and they had been on a visit to Sweden. Wilhelm originally intended to stay in the old country and set up in business but decided to return to America. Jenny and Elin went with them.

The group left Gothenburg by steamer on 5 April 1912 and arrived at Kingston-upon-Hull two days later. From there they travelled to Southampton and boarded RMS *Titanic* on its departure day as third-class passengers. All eight members of the party were lost, and Jenny's body was the only one to be recovered by rescue ship from the ocean. Their grandparents claimed £30,000 in damages.

***

Another tragic story relates to the eight members of the Goodwin family from Melksham in Wiltshire, who all lost their lives in the sinking. Frederick and Augusta Goodwin had intended to travel on another ship, but because of the coal strike they boarded *Titanic* at Southampton as second-class passengers. Their children were Lillian (16), Charles (14), William (11), Jessie (10), Harold (9), and 19-month-old Sidney. They were on their way to a new life with Frederick's brother and his family at Niagara Falls in New York State. Only Sidney's body was recovered from the sea, but it remained unidentified for many years. He was known for nearly 100 years as the 'Unknown Baby' until DNA testing in 2008 proved who he was. There is a memorial to the family at Melksham parish church.

***

Francis Millet was a successful painter, sculptor and writer, and a close friend of Mark Twain, while Major Archibald Butt was military aide to President William Taft. Mr Millet was a veteran of the American Civil War, and Major Butt had seen active service in the Spanish-American War of 1898. They lived together in a large mansion in the Foggy Bottom district of Washington DC, where they were known for throwing lavish parties. A mutual affection was clear to see, and it was said of their relationship, 'The enduring partnership was an early case of "Don't ask, don't tell"' – a rule which was usually followed.

There was some speculation concerning how close the relationship was, and there was gossip that the two men were homosexual. *The New York Times* for 3 March 1912 reported quite distinctly on Major Butt's dandified dress, 'He wore a bright copper-coloured Norfolk jacket fastened by big ball-shaped buttons of red porcelain, a lavender tie, tall bat-wing collar, trousers of the same material as the coat, a derby hat with broad, flat brim, and patent-leather shoes with white tops. The major had a bunch of lilies in his button-hole.'

Pressure of work was affecting Major Butt's health, so on the advice of friends, including Mr Millet and the president, they embarked on a vacation in Europe. After visiting several major cities together, Major Butt went alone to England to visit his brother, and he embarked at Southampton as a first-class passenger, while Francis Millet boarded *Titanic* at Cherbourg later that day. They boarded on separate tickets, with Mr Millet staying in cabin E38, and Major Butt in cabin B38. Frank wrote from Queenstown, 'Queer lot of people on the ship. There are a number of obnoxious, ostentatious American women, the scourge of any place they infest and worse on shipboard than anywhere. Many of them carry tiny dogs, and lead husbands around like pet dogs.'

Both men lost their lives in the disaster, but only Frank's body was recovered. Archibald Gracie gave evidence to the United States Senate inquiry stating that after the ship struck the iceberg, he saw both Butt and Millet in the smoking room in the company of two other men. They were playing cards and making no attempt to save themselves. Lilly Millet, of 'Lilly in a Hammock' or 'Philosophy in Summer' fame, put in a claim of £20,000 for the loss of her husband. In the following year the Butt-Millet Memorial Fountain was erected in their memory, close to the White House in Washington DC.

***

All eight members of the orchestra lost their lives in the disaster. The band leader was Wallace Hartley, who was aged 33 and came from Colne, near Burnley in Lancashire. His body was retrieved from the ocean dressed in his uniform and with his rigid hand still grasping a baton. A few years later his violin and its leather case were found in an attic in England. It had been a gift from his fiancé, Maria Robinson, and after the disaster it had been returned to her from the provincial secretary of Nova Scotia. On her death in 1939, her sister gave it to the Bridlington Brass Band in Yorkshire. It remained in the same family for over seventy years and is now at the Titanic Belfast museum.

The orchestra was made up of Wallace Hartley; John Law Hume (aged 21, from Dumfries); John Wesley Woodward (aged 32, from Oxford); Percy Cornelius Taylor (the only married band member, aged 40, from London); John Frederick Preston Clarke (aged 28, from Liverpool); William Theodore Ronald 'Theo' Brailey (aged 24, from London); Georges Alexandre Krins (aged 23, from Paris); and the youngest member of the band, Roger Marie Bricoux (aged 20, from Burgundy). The bodies of Wallace Hartley, John Hume and John Clarke were recovered by the *Mackay-Bennett*.

Lawrence Beesley, who was rescued in lifeboat 13, remembered:

> I saw a bandsman – the cellist – come round the vestibule corner from the staircase entrance and run down the now deserted starboard deck, his cello trailing behind him, the spike dragging along the floor. This must have been about 12:40am. I suppose the band must have begun to play soon after this and gone on until after 2:00am. Many brave things were done that night, but none more brave than by those few men playing minute after minute as the ship settled quietly lower and lower in the sea and the sea rose higher and higher to where they stood; the music they played serving alike as their own immortal requiem and their right to be recorded on the rolls of undying fame.

Hilda Slayter, who also left the ship in lifeboat 13, stated:

> Of all the heroes who went to their death when the *Titanic* dived to its ocean grave, none deserved greater credit than the members of the vessel's orchestra. The orchestra played until the last. When the vessel took its final plunge the strains of a lively air, mingled gruesomely with

> the cries of those who realised that they were face to face with death. From the moment the vessel struck, or as soon as the members of the orchestra could be collected, there was a steady round of lively airs. It did much to keep up the spirits of everyone and probably served as much as the efforts of the officers trying to prevent panic.

On 30 April 1912, the father of band member Jock Hume received an unsympathetic, now notorious, note from Blacks, which requested: 'We shall be obliged if you will remit us the sum of 5s.4d, which is owing to us as per enclosed statement. We shall also be obliged if you will settle the enclosed uniform account.' The uniform account included items such as lyre lapel insignia and sewing White Star buttons on tunic, and the total bill was 14 shillings and 7 pence.

***

There were at least twelve dogs on the ship. Most of the bigger animals were kept in kennels on F Deck, while others, especially the small ones, were kept in their cabins and out of sight. Several big dogs could be seen being walked regularly along the promenades. There was a King Charles Spaniel and an Airedale Terrier belonging to William and Lucile Carter, along with Mr Carter's polo ponies. There were several birds, including some roosters and hens belonging to Ella White. All the animals, apart from three small dogs, were drowned.

Like most ships, *Titanic* had a cat as a mascot. It was named Jenny and was also expected to help to keep the ship's population of rats and mice in order. Jenny had transferred from *Olympic* and had recently given birth. It has been suggested that Jenny and her kittens had left the ship before she sailed, but Violet Jessop recorded that the cat lived in the galley and: 'laid her family near Jim the scullion, whose approval she always sought and who always gave her warm devotion.'

There were probably more dogs on board, while Charles Moore of Washington DC had made a last-minute change to his plans to transport aboard *Titanic* 100 foxhounds, which he intended to use to start up an English-style foxhunt in the Washington area. They were instead shipped in another vessel.

It was reported that arrangements were being made to hold a dog show during the Monday afternoon of 15 April, and in the evening a concert in aid of the Sailors' Home in Southampton was planned to take place, at which Esther and Eva Hart intended to sing.

***

William Thomas Stead was a well-known investigative journalist, social activist and a strong believer in spiritualism. He believed that he would die at the hands of a lynch mob, or from drowning. He had consulted the celebrated Bond Street palmist Cheiro, who was making a big name for himself because of the accurate prophesies he was expressing. His clients included the Prince of Wales (later King Edward VII), and he foretold the death of Queen Victoria, the circumstances of the death of Lord Kitchener and the abdication of King Edward VIII.

Cheiro warned Mr Stead against travelling over water, especially in the month of April. He stated: 'I see more than a thousand people, you among them, struggling desperately in the water. They are screaming for help and fighting for their lives. But it does none of them any good . . . yourself included!'

In a letter to Mr Stead dated 21 June 1911, Cheiro wrote:

> Yes, I remember very clearly our discussion at lunch here the other day, but I see no reason to go back on what I said then, namely, that as far as I can judge, you need have no reason to believe that your life will end by violence from a London mob.
>
> I have gone over very carefully the impression of your hand that you gave me many years ago, also the more recent notes I made on it, and judging from it and from the date of your birth in the sign of Cancer, otherwise known as the First House of Water, in my humble opinion, any danger of violent death to you must be from water and nothing else. The most important months for you to avoid travelling in are December, and next April of 1912.
>
> Very critical and dangerous for you should be April 1912, especially about the middle of that month. So do not travel by water then if you can help it. If you do you will be liable to meet with such danger to your life that the very worst may happen.
>
> I know I am not wrong with this 'water' danger; I only hope I am, or at least that you will not be travelling somewhere about that period.

Mr Stead is known to have helped people get into the lifeboats, showing no signs of any desire to get into one himself, before he retired to the first-class smoking room, where he was seen sat calmly reading a book as if his death was inevitable.

***

After Benjamin Guggenheim had made certain that Leontine and her maid were safely aboard lifeboat 9, he and his valet Victor Giglio are said to have helped other passengers into the lifeboats. On realising that the situation was very serious, they returned to their cabin and changed into their best evening wear. Titanic survivor Rose Icard wrote in a letter, 'The millionaire Benjamin Guggenheim, after having helped with the rescue of women and children, got dressed and put a rose in his button-hole – to die.'

A steward said Mr Guggenheim lit a cigar and sauntered up to the boat deck to help load the lifeboats. In what was probably his last brave gesture, Mr Guggenheim wrote a letter to his wife, in which he said, 'If anything should happen to me, tell my wife in New York that I have done my best in doing my duty. I played the game straight to the end, and no woman was left on board this ship because Ben Guggenheim was a coward. My last thoughts will be of her and our girls.'

Henry Etches reported: 'Shortly after the last few boats were lowered and I was ordered by the deck officer to man an oar, I waved goodbye to Mr Guggenheim, and that was the last I saw of him.' This could not have been the case because Henry Etches left in the second lifeboat to depart from the ship.

***

Father Thomas Byles had been invited to officiate at his brother William's wedding in New York and had booked a ticket on RMS *Titanic*. He made arrangements with Captain Smith to have the use of space on board to say mass and took a portable altar on the journey for the purpose. On the Sunday morning of 14 April, Father Byles offered what would be his last mass for the passengers. When the ship struck the iceberg, there are many reports that he went about trying to calm the passengers, offering prayers and absolutions. It is also reported that he was offered a place in a lifeboat on two occasions as he helped other passengers climb aboard, but he refused to take a place himself. When all the lifeboats had gone, he is reported to have gone to the end of the boat deck and led a large group of people kneeling around him in prayer.

***

James Clinch Smith was a member of most of New York's elite clubs. He was a skilful yachtsman and a multi-prize-winning rider at the New York Horse Show. He had actually built his own track at Smithtown. His wife Bertha was a well-known musician in the United States and Paris, where she established an all-women orchestra. There had been difficulty in their marriage, but Bertha had contracted tuberculosis, and, after visiting her in Paris, James was on his way back to the States hoping his wife would follow him at a later date. He boarded at Cherbourg and occupied first-class cabin A7. He was an old friend of Colonel Gracie and was one of his 'Our Coterie'. They were table companions, and Colonel Gracie stated that they were together from the beginning to the end of the voyage. The Colonel stated in his book:

> On the night of the terrible disaster when I came up on the deck after having been aroused from my slumbers, I met Smith, and we made an agreement to stick to each other through thick and thin. We first realized the gravity of the situation while we were still on a lower deck when we noticed the list the ship gave toward the port side. We took up our station on the port side of the boat deck, at the bow end, near where women and children were being loaded into one of the boats. Here, without any seeming fear whatsoever, Smith stood, and he and I helped lift women and children and babies over the rail as each boat was loaded and then lowered.
>
> Toward the last, when the list of the vessel became such that Second Officer Lightoller ordered all passengers to the starboard side, Smith at once obeyed and I followed. Here he calmly took in all that was being done by the crew in an attempt to launch a collapsible canvas boat that had been slid down from the hurricane deck, and he and I helped. Before the boat could be launched, the water was upon us.
>
> When Smith and I saw that there was little chance of getting the boat and that it would be overcrowded, when we heard and saw the water rise to the boat deck, we decided to move toward the stern. Still on the starboard side, but our progress was blocked by a mass of humanity, which suddenly appeared from the decks below and consisted of second-class or steerage passengers.
>
> Behind us the water approached rapidly, and we entered a cul-de-sac to which the only outlet was the bridge deck above. Smith tried to reach it by jumping and so did I, but the height was too great for us. The water was now upon us and just as it struck, I rose with a jump at the same time, and was carried high up, when I grasped the brass railing around the bridge deck and held on with might and main. Then I looked hastily to the right and left, but Smith was gone. I never saw him again. Undoubtedly, he was engulfed by the waters and went down with the ship.
>
> Words fail to express the feelings of admiration which I have for his conduct, and the highest tribute I could pay him is this plain recital of what he did in the way of self-sacrifice, knowing no such word as fear in saving the lives of others. His relatives and friends should be proud of him and his record in this terrible disaster.

***

The senior wireless operator Jack Phillips was noted for staying at his post until the very last, and Harold Bride stated:

> Jack Phillips told me that the wireless was growing weaker. The captain came and told us that our engine rooms were taking water and that the dynamos might not last much longer. We sent those facts to the *Carpathia.*
>
> The water was pretty close up to the boat deck. There was a great scramble aft, and how poor Phillips continued to work through it I don't know. He was a brave man. I learned to love him that night and I suddenly felt a great reverence to see him standing there sticking to his work while everybody else was raging about. I will never live to forget the work of Phillips during the last awful fifteen minutes. We picked up the *Olympic* and told her we were sinking by the head.
>
> As Phillips was sending that message, I strapped his lifebelt to his back. I had already put on his overcoat, and I wondered if I could get him into his boots. I saw a collapsible boat near the tunnel and went over to it. Twelve men were trying to boost it down to the boat deck. They were having an awful time. It was the last boat left. I looked at it longingly for a few minutes then I gave them a hand. Over she went, and they all started to scramble in. I walked back to Phillips and said: 'The last raft is gone.'

Tom Whiteley stated, 'Phillips, the first Marconi operator, stuck to his post till the last. He was on the overturned lifeboat with me and was dead when they took him aboard the *Carpathia*. They tried to revive him with brandy and all that, but it was too late. There were four burials at sea on the *Carpathia* – one sailor, two firemen and Phillips.'

***

After the collision, Doctor William O'Loughlin whispered to stewardess Mary Sloan, 'Child, things are very bad.' As the water had reached C Deck, he was seen conversing with Chief Purser Herbert McElroy, Assistant Purser Reginald Barker and Assistant Surgeon L. Edward Simpson. They were joined briefly by Second Officer Lightoller, and as the officer was sweating from his work at the lifeboats, Dr Simpson remarked 'Hello, Lights, are you warm?' They all shook hands with each other, and Purser McElroy is believed to have said, 'Well, goodbye, fellows, it looks like sand for breakfast tomorrow.'

An obituary in the *American Medicine* magazine stated:

> Dr O'Loughlin knew no fear, for he paid no attention to his own danger but went from one group to another, soothing the frightened, encouraging

> the weak and striving in every way to prevent panic and hysteria. As the last lifeboat left the vessel, although he must have known that the end was near, he was see standing in a companionway with the same smile on his face that had endeared him to countless travellers who knew and loved him.

And the *Irish Independent* recorded: 'As an officer of the ship he made no attempt to escape when the accident happened but bent all his energies on helping others. It is said he did not even don a lifebelt. It was a fitting end to an unselfish and self-sacrificing career, one marked at every step by charity, not only that expected by the doctor, but signalled by so liberal giving of money as to leave him usually straightened in his circumstances.'

***

Chief Purser Herbert McElroy was a Liverpudlian who served on the troopship *Britannic* during the 1899–1902 Anglo-Boer War. He was awarded the Troopship Medal and the South Africa Medal with clasp. He was looking after a canary for a Mr Meanwell, and it has been suggested that the bird was taken on board *Titanic* and survived.

The purser was an important post on a ship because his position was one of trust. Passengers came to his office on C Deck near the grand staircase for most things, such as to put in for safe keeping and retrieve valuables, and to hand in wireless messages to pass on to the Marconi room. He would organise repairs when there was a problem in a state room or anywhere else, organise games, sell tickets for such things as the Turkish bath, and take the $1 to purchase a deck chair for the duration of the voyage. After helping at lifeboat 9 he was last seen standing on the boat deck near the gymnasium, next to a mail clerk named William Gwinn.

***

The *Melbourne Argus* for 22 April 1912 ran an article which stated, 'It has been reported in the cable messages that Mr George Eastman, president of the Eastman Kodak Company, is amongst the missing passengers on the *Titanic*.' However, when an obituary for Mr Eastman appeared in a San Francisco newspaper, the Melbourne office of Kodak (Australasia) Limited received a cable message from the head office in Rochester of Mr Eastman's company, stating: - 'Eastman here. No Kodak people on Titanic.'

It appears that George Eastman had been mistaken for a *Titanic* greaser named Charles Eastman, who lost his life in the disaster. He was from Southampton and left a widow and seven children un-provided for. His brother-on-law, Charles Perren, who was a second-class boots steward, was also lost in the sinking.

***

A conman tried to use the tragedy to his advantage by faking his own death to escape justice. He was Jay Yates, who was known to the police and in sporting circles as J.H. Rogers. He was thought to have been travelling on *Titanic* and was hailed as a hero for helping women and children into the lifeboats. He was believed to have given the following message to one of the women he had helped: 'If saved, inform my sister, Mrs J.F. Adams of Findlay, Ohio. Lost.' He signed it as J.H. Rogers.

In fact, Yates was never on board the liner, and he had used the disaster to fake his own death because he was wanted by the police. He had written the hoax note in New York and got a woman to pose as a survivor and take it to a newspaper. The police did not fall for the ruse, and he was later arrested in connection with postal thefts while using yet another fake name.

***

On 18 April a New York newspaper reported: 'The captain of the steamship *La Bretagne*, which has arrived here, reports that on the voyage across the Atlantic he saw huge icebergs. Forty polar bears were seen clinging to the surfaces of the giant bergs.'

A German ship named *Clio* reported sighting a broken iceberg 130 feet high, carrying saloon fittings, chairs, hand-bags, cushions and wreckage believed to have formed part of *Titanic*.

On arriving in New York on 24 April, the officers of the North German Lloyd steamer *Princess Irene* stated: 'The wireless operator intercepted a despatch in which some ships reported, in passing a spot approximately 50 miles from the scene of the Titanic disaster, that they had sighted an iceberg on which were the bodies of more than a dozen men wearing lifebelts. The opinion of the officers was that the men climbed on the mass of ice and had frozen to death. No attempt was made to take the bodies off.'

The White Star Line contracted four vessels to search for bodies in the area of the sea where *Titanic* sank. A cable-repair ship based at

Halifax in Nova Scotia, Canada, called the CS *Mackay-Bennett*, sailed from Halifax on 21 April and searched the disaster area a few days later.

Newspapers reported:

> 'A Gruesome Titanic Story. What the Funeral Ship Saw: The first man to land from the funeral ship which was sent out from New York to recover bodies was Mr John Snow, who superintended the work of embalming the dead, and generally directed the caring for the bodies as they were recovered from the ocean.
>
> Among the bodies recovered is that of a two-year-old baby boy. He came floating to us with upturned face. His was the only body recovered which had no lifebelt. Nothing I have ever seen at sea made such an impression on me.
>
> We secured about 40 miles from the scene of the disaster the bodies of twelve women. It has been stated that there was an explosion in the sinking *Titanic*, and this probably explains the terribly mutilated condition of many of the bodies. Arms and legs were shattered and faces and bodies mangled. We picked up many lifebelts 170 miles from the wreck.
>
> Many of the bodies were of persons in full evening dress. All the watches worn by the men had stopped at precisely ten minutes past 2. There was hardly any variation.
>
> We recovered in all 306 bodies, buried 116 at sea, and have brought home 190. There was evidence of a fierce struggle for life in some cases. Hands were clutching clothing, and faces were distorted with terror. Ours was a terrible task.
>
> There was a special service for each body buried at sea, the hymn, 'Jesu, Lover of my Soul' being sung. We found and photographed the black iceberg which caused the wreck. It was an immense berg, but badly shattered.
>
> As soon as the ship was docked, Captain Richard Roberts, commander of Mr Astor's yacht, went on board, and a coffin was pulled away from a pile on the after deck, and opened. Mr Roberts looked in. 'That is Colonel Astor,' he said. The body was dressed in blue suit and had been found encased in a life-belt, and floating in an upright position. Round the waist was a gold buckle, and in the pockets £500 in notes and cash.
>
> By far the greater number of the bodies recovered were floating in groups of 20 or more amid the debris. Buoyed up by their cork belts, the bodies at a distance looked like a flock of gulls at rest on the water. Like Mr Astor, they were all in an upright position, as if treading water.
>
> Most of the recovered victims were buried in two separate mass graves in Fairview Lawn Cemetery at Halifax, while others were claimed by their families from around the world and transported for repatriation.

The Western Union's CS *Minia* left Halifax on 22 April and because of bad weather, it only recovered seventeen bodies, all apparently miles apart from each other. As the ship was searching the area where the disaster occurred, Captain William De Carteret took a picture of an iceberg and stated that a long red streak which could be clearly seen along its side indicated a possible collision with an ocean liner. However, the German ship SMS *Prinz Adalbert* had set sail on 15 April, and the *Titanic* disaster was still unknown to the members of its crew. Visibility was clear, and the chief steward of the liner *M Linoenewald*, noticed a huge red streak on an iceberg, as if something had dragged against it, and the steward took a photograph of it. Could there have been two icebergs with red streaks, or was it the same iceberg? After studying both photographs, the two icebergs look different, and the CS *Minia* photograph matches the descriptions by the survivors of the disaster more accurately. Perhaps the red streak is some kind of natural phenomenon?

The *Montmagny* left Halifax on 6 May and picked up four bodies; and on 25 May an Irish saloon steward named James McGrady was the only body saved from the sea by the SS *Algernine*, after three weeks of searching.

A bedroom steward from Dorset named William Thomas Kerly was picked up by the tanker SS *Ottawa* on 6 June, and fifty-four days after the disaster, the last body was retrieved from the icy waters. It was clad in a lifejacket and had drifted 375 miles from the wreck site. The body was that of first-class saloon steward William Frederick Cheverton and was picked up by the SS *Ilford* on 8 June. A Royal Navy veteran, his body was buried at sea.

On the first anniversary of the disaster, an Australian newspaper reported:

> Mr W.F. Bassett, chief officer on the steamer *Ilford*, which arrived at Newcastle yesterday from Moji, gave a representative of the *Newcastle Morning Herald* an interesting account of the discovery by him of the body of one of the victims of the *Titanic* disaster. Yesterday was the anniversary of that awful calamity.
>
> On June 8 last year, when the *Ilford* was in latitude 46.06 north, longitude 42.51 west, bound from Galveston to Hamburg, Mr Bassett was on the bridge at about noon, when his attention was attracted by an object in the water. On using the glasses, he saw that it was a body. The steamer was stopped and a boat lowered with Mr Bassett and the third officer and two seamen.
>
> On recovering the body, it was found to be encircled by a lifebelt and from letters, postcards and Christmas cards found in the pockets of the

> clothing it was ascertained that it was that of W.F. Cheverton, a steward on the ill-fated *Titanic*. A watch and chain, bunch of keys, knife and silver pencil case were also found, and these were handed over to the British Consul in Hamburg for despatch to the deceased's relatives in England, at the address shown in the letters.
>
> The body after the removal of the articles mentioned from the pockets was weighted and consigned to the deep. It had been in the water for 54 days and carried by the Gulf Stream at the rate of seven miles a day to where it was found.

On 10 June it was reported under the heading: 'Floating Lifeboat: Mystery of the Sea' that 'The German steamer *Essenbach*, while on her voyage to this port (Baltimore), sighted a barnacle-covered lifeboat near the scene of the *Titanic* disaster. The master of the *Essenbach* did not deem it worth his while to examine the boat, so that it is unknown as to whether there were any bodies on board.'

In mid-July 1931 it was reported from New York: 'After having washed about in the sea for 19 years, a lifebelt marked 'SS *Titanic*' was washed up on the shore of Gravesend Bay, New York, recently.'

***

There have been various accounts of Captain Smith's last moments concerning the disaster, and it is almost certain that if his distinctive body and uniform was found, it would have been identified, which it was not, and there is no definite evidence that Captain Smith lost his life on that day.

At the United States inquiry, Harold Bride stated that when they were launching the collapsible boats five minutes before the ship went down, he saw Captain Smith jump overboard from the Bridge, which by that time was very low in the water. He was not wearing a lifejacket.

At least three eyewitnesses, a passenger named Charles Eugene Williams, in lifeboat 14, and two crew members named Harry Senior and Walter 'Wally' Hurst, both in collapsible B, say they saw the captain in the water as the lifeboats were trying to get away from the doomed liner, and Williams said he actually had a short conversation with him.

Charles Williams went overboard with a life preserver when he could no longer stay on deck. He was in the icy water for over two hours before he was finally hauled into one of the lifeboats. He says that he saw Captain Smith swimming around with an infant in his arms and a lifebelt. When the small boat went to his rescue, Captain

Smith handed them the child but refused to get in himself. He asked what had become of First Officer Murdoch, to which he was told that he had blown his brains out with a revolver. 'Then Captain Smith pushed himself away from the lifeboat, threw his lifebelt from him and slowly sank from sight. He did not come to the surface again.'

Fireman Harry Senior said he saw the captain swim back to the ship after he had rescued the baby. He stated, 'The ship was pretty near sinking then, and the captain shouted, "Each man for himself." I had noticed him on the Bridge before that. He was pacing up and down sending up rockets and giving orders.' When the captain's order came, Senior dived over the side. He continued, 'As I was swimming to the boat I saw the captain in the water. He was swimming with a baby in his arms, raising it out of the water as he swam on his back. He swam to a boat, put the baby in, and then swam back to the ship. I also had picked up a baby, but it died from the cold before I could reach the boat.'

Walter 'Wally' Hurst and his father-in-law, William Mintram, served as firemen on the ship. They met each other shortly before *Titanic* went down. William had a lifejacket and he gave it to his son-in-law. This act of selfless courage probably cost William his life and may well have contributed to the fact that Walter was able to stay on the upturned collapsible B and survive.

Walter's daughter Rosina related: 'My father was one of the last ones off and he was in the collapsible boat that was upside down in the water, he was on the top of that, and he always said that, you know the captain of the ship, they say all sorts of things about what happened to him, well he said somebody swam up to the boat and he couldn't get on because there was so many on there, and he said "Good luck, boys" and he went. My dad swore it was the captain that said that.'

It is known that Officer Lowe rescued at least four men from the water when he returned to the area of the disaster, and one of them died. One of the other three may have been an Italian named Emilio Portaluppi. However, there is stronger evidence to suggest that Mr Portaluppi was rescued in lifeboat 4. If that is so, who was this fourth man? Others, such as Emily Ryerson, suggested they picked up as many as six or seven men.

Captain Smith must have been in the icy water for quite a long time, so would he have been in any conscious state to say who he was, and would he have been recognisable, especially in the dark? Officer Lowe and Fireman Tom Threlfall were in the boat, but Lowe was preoccupied organising the rescue attempt and Tom was busy looking after one of the female passengers.

It is believed that a survivor was picked up by *Carpathia* and seemingly rushed away from the eyes of those around him. Who was this man?

Some suggest it was Bruce Ismay. However, at least one passenger, Jack Thayer, was allowed to go into his cabin and speak to him, so what would have been the point of getting him away from the others and then let him be seen? It is also known that the survivors of the crew were not disembarked with the passengers, but were taken by a tender, the *George Starr*, at Pier 61. There seems to have been an attempt to keep the crew away from awkward questions until they had been briefed. The root of all evil also raised its head. According to the *London Daily News*, one of the things the Senate inquiry intended to find out was: 'Why a Marconi company's official sent a wireless to the operator on *Carpathia* on Thursday, stating: "Say nothing. Hold your story for dollars in four figures."'

For more information on the fate of Captain Smith see Chapter 9 – 'Did Captain Smith Survive the Sinking?' from *Unlucky Seven: The Story of the Ill-Fated Liner's Officers.*

FOR GALLANTRY

Many people have tried to find a pattern to the type of person who gains a gallantry award – without success. We may sometimes wonder how we would cope in a life-or-death situation. 'What about my family if I do not survive?' or "What if I am maimed?' Given time to consider the consequences, a person might well hesitate and decide not to get involved. However, such incidents usually occur at the spur of the moment, the adrenaline flows, and the natural reaction is to act without thinking of one's own safety.

Many brave acts were performed during the evacuation of RMS *Titanic,* but no official British recognitions were ever awarded. It has to be understood that not all the brave acts performed that night fit the criteria for the awards available at that time. For instance, although the band showed great courage in playing on as the ship sank, as far as it is known none of them physically helped to save any lives. However, some members of the crew certainly did, and based on the knowledge I have attained from studying the criteria for gallantry awards over five decades, I believe the following officers who went beyond the call of duty would have been considered:

Chief Officer Henry Tingle Wilde (posthumous) – RMS *Titanic*
First Officer William McMaster Murdoch (posthumous) – RMS *Titanic*
Second Officer Charles Herbert Lightoller – RMS *Titanic*
Third Officer Herbert John Pitman – RMS *Titanic*
Fourth Officer Joseph Groves Boxhall – RMS *Titanic*
Fifth Officer Harold Godfrey Lowe – RMS *Titanic*
Sixth Officer James Paul Moody (posthumous) – RMS *Titanic*
Captain Arthur Henry Rostron – CS *Carpathia*

Captain Rostron received the United States Congressional Medal of Honour, which is presented for 'national appreciation for distinguished achievements and contributions by individuals or institutions.'

The Board of Trade's Sea Gallantry Medal for Foreign Service was instituted in 1841 for foreigners (non-Brits) who saved lives from British vessels. It was awarded in gold, silver and bronze. Officially it was awarded 'for saving the life of a British subject or assisting a British vessel in distress.' Then the Merchant Shipping Act of 1854 provided for rewards to lifesavers, which led to the creation of the Board of Trade Medal for Saving Life at Sea in the following year, which became known as the Sea Gallantry Medal (SGM). They were struck in gold, silver and bronze, but only the latter two were ever awarded.

The medal was to be presented to those 'affording assistance towards the preservation of life and property in cases of shipwreck and distress at sea.' In 1887, the year of Queen Victoria's golden jubilee, the Board of Trade further defined the award as 'for the rescue of life from shipwreck on the coast of the United Kingdom, whether the ship is British or foreign', as well as for 'the rescue of life from British vessels in more distant seas.' Therefore, in practice, it was awarded to seafarers serving with British-registered merchant ships. It could be given for both individual gallantry and for collective cases of heroism, such as to each member of a ship's crew. Awards could be made posthumously. It was last bestowed in 1989 and although it has not been officially abolished, it, along with the foreign-service version, which was last awarded in 1968, seems to have fallen into disuse.

The Albert Medal was instituted on 7 March 1866 to reward gallantry in saving life at sea, and was named by Queen Victoria in memory of her beloved Albert, the Prince Consort, who had died in 1861. An amendment in 1867 created first and second classes of the medal and ten years later the scope of the award was extended to gallantry in saving life on land. The title of the award was altered in 1917; the first class becoming the Albert Medal in Gold and the second class simply the Albert Medal.

The award was ceased in 1971 and surviving holders were invited to exchange their medal for the George Cross. The criteria for the award of George Cross being: 'For acts of the greatest heroism of the most conspicuous courage in circumstances of extreme danger.' However, none of the people who may have been eligible for the award of Albert Medal for gallantry during the RMS *Titanic* disaster lived long enough to have exchanged it for the George Cross.

The following narratives represent the type of incidents for which the Albert Medal has been awarded:

> The Queen [Victoria] has been graciously pleased to confer the decoration of the Albert Medal of a 2nd Class upon A.B. William Carter

of the barque *Gettysburg*, of Aberdeen. The following is an account of the services in respect on which the decoration has been conferred.

The *Gettysburg* was lost by striking on the Morant Cays [off Jamaica] on the night between 31 March and 1 April 1889, while on a voyage from Montevideo to Pensacola, seven of the crew being drowned. The sea during the night washed over the ship and over the remaining nine of the crew, who, however, managed to hang on to the wreck until daylight, when William Carter and seven men managed to reach a rock, which was seen above water at a distance of about 500 yards. The master of the vessel tried to follow, but was injured and exhausted, and the sea was so strong that he was knocked down and would have been drowned had not Carter returned and carried him to the rock. Carter afterwards swam out and secured part of the top mast and yard, lashed them together, and with assistance brought them ashore, where they were formed into a raft.

The nine men left got on the raft and with small pieces of wood commenced to paddle to the nearest island, a distance of one and a half miles, Carter and another seaman at times swimming alongside and directing the raft, which was frequently turned off its course and sometimes upset owing to the heavy sea which was running at the time. Carter and six others subsequently swam to a larger island a quarter of a mile distant, the former returning the next day and assisting the master and a seaman, who were seriously injured, to reach it.

The survivors of the shipwrecked crew remained on the large island till the 21st of April, when Carter and others manufactured a larger raft, on which two of the crew sailed to Jamaica, a distance of 32 miles, in two days, whereby the rescue of all the men was ultimately affected.

Another example read:

The Queen [Victoria] has conferred the decoration of the Albert Medal of the Second Class on John Dinneen, chief mate of the steamship *Albatross*, of London. The following is an account of the services in respect of which the decoration has been conferred.

On 4 November 1888, the schooner *Isabella Hall* of Barrow, stranded on the Tongue Sands [in the Thames Estuary], and the crew, having lost their boat in a heavy sea, were obliged to take to the rigging and wait for assistance.

Next morning, two boats were despatched from two different steamers to their relief but could not get near to the wreck, owing to the heaviness of the sea, and the shipwrecked crew were in danger of losing their lives, when the steamship *Albatross* of London, which was passing up channel, despatched a boat, manned by the chief mate John Dinneen, and four seamen, who, not withstanding strong warnings from the other boats of the danger of the attempt, rowed close to the wreck, and after nearly an hour's struggle, threw a line on board and rescued one of the crew.

He was scarcely got into the boat when a heavy sea nearly swamped her, and washed Dinneen and three seamen out of her. They, however, managed to regain the boat and, bailing her out, proceeded with their task, and finally succeeded in rescuing the remainder of the shipwrecked men. The service throughout was attended with very great risk and difficulty, and owed its success chiefly to the energy and determination of Dinneen, and his constant encouragement of his men.

The Board of Trade have also awarded a piece of plate to Captain James Brown Randall, master of the *Albatross,* for his humanity and kindness to the shipwrecked crew on the occasion, and their silver medal for gallantry [Sea Gallantry Medal] to the four seamen – W. King, H. Fedder, R. Lacy and A. Oakley, who manned the rescuing boat of the *Albatross*.

Appendix

A GIANT ICY FINGER OF DEATH

Under the heading 'A Giant Icy Finger of Death Rose Out of the Sea to Point a Moral Dilemma: The Story of the *Titanic* Disaster' the *Daily Mirror* published a special feature on New Years Eve of 1947:

'On the morning of April 10, 1912, a small group of seamen stood on the wharf at Southampton swearing a little among themselves as a giant liner out in the stream slowly turned her bows and headed towards the open waters of the English Channel. They were stokers who had missed their ship, and they were angry men, for this was no ordinary voyage; it was the maiden voyage of the largest ship ever built, the mighty colossus of the seas, pride of Britain's White Star fleet, the marine marvel of the age - the great steamship *Titanic*.

For two years the world had been intrigued by the building of the mammoth vessel, marvelling at the statistics of her size and the ingenuity of her designers and constructors. Doubts as to whether such a gigantic vessel could be made seaworthy had been set at rest by emphatic claims that she was absolutely unsinkable, that her double bottom, and the division of the hull into 16 great watertight compartments made her invulnerable to any hazard of the sea.

Now with her maiden voyage, history was being made, and the tardy stokers cursed their mates who had refused to raise the lowered gangway to put them aboard her. Within a week, however, they were thanking their lucky stars for being left stranded on the wharf, for at 2:20am on April 15 the world was shocked by the news that the great *Titanic* was at the bottom of the sea, two hours and 40 minutes after striking a gigantic iceberg while on her way across the Atlantic to New York.

Shock turned to stricken horror when it was later revealed that 1,490 of the 2,201 souls on board had gone down with her. And horror turned to angry conjecture when it was learned that the vessel was travelling at high speed in waters dangerously close to the region of Arctic ice when disaster struck. In the days and weeks which followed this, one of the greatest sea disasters of all time, anguished relatives and friends of those who had died, and newspapers on both sides of the Atlantic asked many indignant and pertinent questions why had *Titanic* been allowed to sail with lifeboat accommodation sufficient only for about half the passengers and crew? And why had some boats been allowed to leave the stricken liner only half-full – and in some cases less than half-full?

Why had the ship been driven at almost top speed – 22 knots – in a known region of icebergs? Why had not the passengers been told the full seriousness of the situation when the vessel first struck, instead of having been left with the impression that the lowering of the boats was only a precautionary measure?

There were other questions, too, with uglier implications. In the loading of the boats, had there been discrimination between the classes, with the result that a considerably higher proportion of first class than third class passengers had been saved?

Had the survivors in some of the half-filled boats deliberately and callously refrained from attempting the rescue of others struggling in the water after the ship went down?

Answers to these and many other questions were sought at two exhaustive inquiries, one conducted by the British Board of Trade, the governing body of the British mercantile marine, and the other by a committee of the United States Senate.

Apart from the obvious need for adequate lifeboat and life raft accommodation in every ship that puts to sea, the most outstanding lesson of the *Titanic* disaster was the immeasurable value at sea of the then newly-invented wireless telegraphy. Had it not been for wireless, which at that time had only recently been installed in some ships, the *Titanic* death-roll would have been much longer, for most, if not all, of the survivors in the boats would have died from exposure and exhaustion if they had been forced to drift for many more hours than they did.

Throughout that fatal voyage, by the melty of providence, the sea was calm and the weather fine, but after leaving the last port of call – Queenstown, Ireland – it became steadily colder.

The course set was the usual "great circle" route followed by large ships on the westbound Atlantic run. It lay about 25 miles south of, or outside, the area marked on the charts as being a region of field ice between March and July, but 100 to 300 miles north of, or inside the area marked icebergs have been seen within this line in April, May and June.

When the actual presence of ice in the shipping lanes was first wirelessed by the SS *Caronia* at 9am on Sunday, April 14, the position given by the *Caronia* was more than 12 hours steaming ahead of the *Titanic*.

However, even after the liner entered the region stated, the master, Captain Smith (who went down with the ship) did not order a slackening of speed. His lack of precaution in that respect was sharply criticised, and one of the findings of the British court of inquiry was that the speed of the vessel at the time of the collision was "excessive in the circumstances." Although he was deemed to have made a "mistake" in this, he was not adjudged guilty of negligence.

In Captain Smith's defence it was pointed out that nine out of ten skippers in that era of intense shipping competition would have done just what he did – posted a lookout man and continued at the same speed. The odds against a ship striking an iceberg in that latitude at that time of the year were estimated and used as an official basis by marine insurance companies as a million to one.

Several other ice warnings came crackling over the *Titanic's* wireless that fatal Sunday, the last at 9:40pm, only two hours steaming from the position where the liner went to her death. This last message reported much heavy pack ice and a great number of icebergs, also field ice, in approximately that same position. But the message never reached the Bridge. The wireless operator was trying to cope with a flood of passengers' messages for transmission through Cape Race, Newfoundland, and he apparently placed, the ice-warning message to one side, and forgot about it.

In the meantime, the ordinary shipboard routine had proceeded smoothly. Most of the passengers drifted off to bed between 10 and 11pm. Captain Smith had retired to his cabin, and on the Bridge, temporarily in command, was First Officer W.M. Murdoch, who had relieved the Second Officer C.H. Lightoller at 10 pm. All was quiet on the dimly-lighted Bridge except for an occasional quiet order by Murdoch to the helmsman.

Ahead, all was darkness, for it was a moonless night. Time crept on until it was within 20 minutes of midnight. Suddenly the bell from the lookout man's post in the crow's nest rang urgently three times. Murdoch knew what that meant – "obstacle dead ahead." Almost simultaneously the frantic voice of the lookout man came over the crow's nest telephone: "Iceberg! Right ahead!"

The First Officer, reacting to the signal automatically and instantaneously, had already shouted "Hard a-starboard" to the helmsman and whipped the handle of the engine-room telegraph first to "Stop" and then to "Full astern." With agonising slowness, the bow of the great ship, still surging forward under her own momentum, swung two points to port. The seconds ticked away as the helmsman strained at the spokes of the wheel, while Murdoch held his breath. The next instant the starboard side of the *Titanic* forward met the great menacing wall of the 'berg in a glancing blow and the liner shuddered to a stop. Great chunks of ice crashed on to the foredeck as the iceberg, like some monstrous silent animal of the night, slipped away into the darkness as suddenly as it had appeared. Yet so slight was the glancing impact that scarcely one sleeper was awakened, and of those passengers who were still awake not one realised that there had been a serious collision. But within a few minutes of the collision, Captain Smith, who had gone immediately to the Bridge, and his officers knew that the damage was very serious – knew, in fact, that the ship was mortally stricken.

A hasty examination far below in the regions of the stokeholds and mail rooms revealed the almost unbelievable fact that the mere ten seconds of contact between ship and iceberg had been sufficient to rip a gash below the water-line 300 feet long – more than one-third of the entire length of the ship. And the icy sea was pouring through the breach in a steady flood.

The passengers were ordered to assemble on deck wearing their lifebelts. Bewildered, rather than alarmed at first, they did so. By this time the safety valves on the huge funnels were lifted, and the roar of escaping steam was deafening.

An order had been passed to the wireless room, and the Morse key was chattering out a stream of "CQD, CQD, CQD" followed by the position of the liner. Later that tragic night the old distress signal CQD was changed to the newly-adopted international call of SOS. The call for assistance was picked up by Cape Race and by half a dozen ships. The nearest was the *Mount Temple*, only 50 miles away, but unfortunately on the opposite side of the great field of ice the outer edge of which the *Titanic* had struck.

The *Carpathia* was 58 miles away in another direction. Her captain replied at once, ordered a double watch in the stokehold, and steered at full speed towards the *Titanic's* position, risking a collision with an iceberg in order to get there as fast as he could.

There was one other ship much nearer – the *Californian*, but she carried only one wireless operator and he had gone off duty only ten minutes before the *Titanic* struck the ice field. Nevertheless, the behaviour of the *Californian*'s master was hard to understand and was severely criticised at the subsequent inquiries. The *Californian* was hove-to less than 10 miles from the *Titanic* because of the danger of collision with the same ice field. The *Titanic*'s distress rockets were seen from her Bridge, but although Morse signals were flashed in reply no attempt was made to send her to the *Titanic*'s assistance. The failure of the *Californian*'s master in this respect amounted to "culpable negligence," according to the British court of inquiry.

Many of the *Titanic*'s passengers were bemused by the vessel's reputation of being "unsinkable" and the ship's officers had great difficulty in persuading the passengers that the situation was really serious when the order came for them to take to the boats. Moreover, there had been no boat drill and the organisation for getting the boats away was deplorably deficient.

From the boat deck to the dark sea, it was a drop of 65 feet, and many women were afraid to enter the boats swinging at the davits; others refused to leave their husbands. As the tension mounted, panic gripped the more excitable section of the European emigrants in the steerage class, and an officer was compelled to fire a few revolver shots over their heads to stop a rush for the boats. Despite the confusion, the unnerving roar of escaping steam, and the mounting fear as it became apparent from the firing of rockets and the steady settling towards the bow that the *Titanic* was sinking, the behaviour of the vast majority of the passengers was admirable, and there were many gallant and touching scenes.

Among the many stories of quiet courage in the face of death is that of several men who, right up to the last awful plunge, remained in the ship's gymnasium sparring at punching bags and riding stationary bicycles.

Among the crew perhaps the most impressive behaviour at that testing time was that of the band, the members of which remained on deck playing to the end. At first they played "ragtime" and popular tunes; then, as the end drew near, they changed to the hymn "Nearer my God to Thee," and many of the passengers, joined in singing the words while others knelt to pray.

Except for one or two who panicked, the stokers heroically continued working in the stokeholds not flooded, to keep up steam for the dynamos supplying the wireless and lighting plants with current.

Just before 2am the haggard captain entered the wireless room where Chief Operator Phillips and his assistant, Harold Bride, were still hammering out the endless "SOS, SOS,

SOS." Smith told them that they could do no more and it was now "every man for himself."

To those in the boats the death-plunge of the great liner was an awful sight. Every light was blazing almost up to the last moment. Then they went out, only to flicker on again just as the dying ship reared itself up like a living monster in its death agonies and remained for a minute or more motionless in the perpendicular position before the final plunge. As she stood poised above the dark sea, the survivors heard a frightful, crashing roar lasting about 20 seconds as the machinery tore loose from its foundations, and with every movable object on the ship crashed down into the submerged bow in a chaotic cascade.

In the meantime, the *Carpathia,* steaming under forced draught, was speeding to the rescue. She arrived at the scene of the disaster at 4am and picked up the first boatload of survivors five minutes later. The other boats were scattered over four or five miles of sea, and the *Carpathian* work of succour was not completed until 8 am, by which time all the boats had been found and 712 persons (one of whom died on the voyage to New York) had been rescued.

The sacrifice of the 1,490 men, women and children who lost their lives on the *Titanic* was not entirely in vain. Today, as a direct result of the *Titanic* tragedy, no ocean-going vessel leaves port without lifeboats and life-rafts sufficient for all on board, or without a continuous wireless service. It was a costly lesson.'

BIBLIOGRAPHY AND RESEARCH SOURCES

Acron Beacon Journal, 20 April 1912
American Medicine Magazine, 1912
Atlantic Daily Bulletin, the Journal of the British Titanic Society
Australian National Maritime Museum

Babler, Gunter, *Guide to the Crew of Titanic: The Structure of Working aboard the Legendary Liner*, 2017
Ballard, Robert Duane, *the Discovery of the Titanic*, 1987
Bancroft, James W., *Local Heroes: Tributes to Bravery*, 1992
Bancroft, James W., *Devotion to Duty: A Victorian Military and Naval History Trilogy*, 1994
Bancroft, James W., *Titanic: Iceberg Ahead. The Story of the Disaster by Some of Those Who Were There*, 2021
Bancroft, James W., *Titanic Disaster: Omens, Mysteries and Misfortunes of the Doomed Liner*, 2023
Bancroft, James W., *Unlucky Seven: The Story of the Ill-Fated Liner's Officers*, 2024
Bancroft, James W., *Lightoller: Titanic to Dunkirk*, 2024
Bancroft, James W., *Titanic: Greater Manchester Connections*, 2025
Bath Chronicle, 4 and 11 May 1912
Beavis, Debbie, *Who Sailed on Titanic: The Definitive Passenger List*, 2002
Beed, Blair Stephen, *Titanic Victims in Halifax Graveyards*, 2001
Beesley, Lawrence, *the Loss of the SS Titanic: Its Story and Its Lessons*, 1912
Behe, George, *On Board RMS Titanic: Memories of the Maiden Voyage*, 2012
Behe, George, *the Triumvirate: Captain Edward J Smith, Bruce Ismay, Thomas Andrews and the Sinking of Titanic*, 2024
Belfast Irish Weekly, 15 March 1907
Belfast Telegraph, 15 April 1912 and 22 March 2025
Belfast Titanic Society

Beveridge, Bruce; and Hall, Steve, *RMS Titanic in 50 Objects: With Images of Artefacts from the Collection of White Star Memories*, 2022

Bile, Serge, *Black Man on the Titanic: The Story of Joseph Laroche*, 2019

Birmingham Mail, 20 June 1913

Board of Trade: *The Investigation into the Loss of the* SS *Titanic*, 1912

Boxhall, Joseph Groves, diary dated from 1899 to 1902

Boxhall, Commander Joseph, Transcript of BBC Radio broadcast on 22 October 1962

Brainerd Daily Dispatch, 2 December 1937

Brewster, Hugh, *Gilded Lives, Fatal Voyage: The Titanic's Fist Class Passengers and Their World*, 2012

Bristol Times and Mirror, 27 April 1912

British Government: *Loss of the Steamship Titanic: Report of a Formal Investigation into the Circumstances Attending the Foundering on April 15, 1912 of the British Steamship Titanic, of Liverpool, After Striking Ice in or near Latitude 41 - 46 N; Longitude 50 – 14 W, North Atlantic Ocean, as Conducted by the British Government*, 1912

British Titanic Society

Broken Hill Barrier Miner (NSW), 4 May 1934

Brooklyn Daily Eagle, 19 April 1912

Bullock, Shan F: *A Titanic Hero: Thomas Andrews, Shipbuilder*, 1912

Butler, Daniel Allen, *Unsinkable: The Full Story of RMS Titanic*, 1998

Cameron, Stephen, *Titanic: Belfast's Own*, 1998

Canberra Times, 18 October 1962 and 6 October 1985

Chicago Inter Ocean, 21 April 1912

Chirnside, Mark, *The 'Olympic' Class Ships: Olympic, Titanic and Britannic*, 2011

Chirnside, Mark, T*the Sting of the Hawke: Collision in the Solent. The Full Story Behind the Collision between HMS* Hawke *and RMS* Olympic *on 20 September 1911*, 2015

Chirnside, Mark, *The Big Four of the White Star Fleet: Celtic, Cedric, Baltic and Adriatic*, 2016

Chirnside, Mark, *Oceanic: White Star's Ship of the Century*, 2018

Colliers Magazine, 4 May 1912

Cooper, Gary J., *Titanic Captain: The Life of Edward John Smith*, 2011

Cornwall, Thomas, *Titanic: The John B (Jack) Thayer Chronicles*, 2019

Daily Commercial News and Shipping List, Sydney, 21 November 1910

Daily Mirror, 13 May 1912, 31 December 1947 and 23 April 2017

Daily Sketch, 4 May 1912

Davenport-Hines, Richard: *Titanic Lives: Migrants and Millionaires, Conmen and Crew*, 2012

Davie, Michael, *Titanic: The Full Story of the Tragedy*, 1986
Dundalk Democrat, 27 June 1912

Encyclopaedia Titanica
Everett, Marshall, *Wreck and Sinking of the Titanic, the Oceans Greatest Disaster*, 1912

Fitch, Tad; Layton, J. Kent; and Wormstedt, Bill, *On a Sea of Glass: The life and Loss of RMS Titanic*, 2015
Folkestone Herald, 4 May 1912

Gannon, Joe, *Titanic Hero Hugh McElroy: Sand for Breakfast Tomorrow*, 2018
Gannon, Robert, *What Really Sank the Titanic, Popular Science*, February 1995
Geller, Judith B., *Titanic: Women and Children First*, 1998
General Register Office: Index of Births, Marriages and Deaths
Gibbons, Elizabeth, *To the Bitter End*, 1992
Gibbs, Lindsay, *Titanic: The Tennis Story*, 2012
Gibbs, Phillip, *Deathless Story of the Titanic: Lloyds Weekly News*, 1912
Goldsmith, Frank John William, *Echoes in the Night: Memories of a Titanic Survivor*, 1991
Grace's Guide to British Industrial History
Gracie, Archibald, *Truth about the Titanic*, 1973
Grafton Daily Examiner (NSW), 3 May 1937

Halpern, Samuel, *Report into the Loss of the SS Titanic: A Centennial Appraisal*, 2011
Harland & Wolff Director's Minute Book held in the Public Records Office
Harris, Rene, *Her Husband Went Down with the* Titanic, *Liberty Magazine*, 23 April 1932
Harper's Weekly, 27 April 1912
Holman, Hannah, *Titanic Voices: 63 Survivors Tell Their Extraordinary Stories*, 2011
Horswill, Albert, 'Headlines of Other Days', Radio broadcast, 10 May 1934
Houston Chronicle, 13 April 2012
Hull Daily Mail, 15, 18 and 20 April 1912
Hyslop, Donald; Forsyth, Alastair; Jemima, Sheila, *Titanic Voices: Memories from the Fateful Voyage*, 1994

Imperial War Museum, London
Ismay, Clifford, *Understanding J Bruce Ismay: The True Story of the Man they Called 'The Coward of the Titanic'*, 2022

Jewish Journal, 29 March 2012
JWB Historical Archive

Lancashire Evening Post, 16 November 2024
Lancashire Life, January 2025
Larne Times, 27 April 1912
Lightoller, Charles Herbert, *Titanic and Other Ships*, 1935
Liverpool Journal of Commerce, 9 August 1912
Liverpool Record Office
Lives of the First World War, 1914–1918
Lloyds List
Lord, Walter, *A Night to Remember*, 1955
Lord, Walter, *The Night Lives On: Thoughts, Theories and Revelations about the Titanic*, 1986

Marcus, Geoffrey Jules, *The Maiden Voyage*, 1969
Manchester Guardian, July 1932
McCarty, Jennifer Hooper; and Foecke, Tim, *What Really Sank the Titanic: New Forensic Discoveries*, 2008
Marshall, Logan, *The Sinking of the Titanic and Great Sea Disasters*, 1912
Medhurst, Simon, *Titanic Day by Day: 366 Days with the Titanic*, 1922
Merseyside Maritime Museum
Moss, Michael S. and John R. Hume, *Shipbuilders to the World: 125 Years of Harland and Wolf, Belfast, 1861–1986*, 1986
Mowbray, Jay Henry, *Sinking of the Titanic: Thrilling Stories Told by Survivors*, 1912
Myers, L.T., *the Sinking of the Titanic and Great Sea Disasters. Thrilling Stories of Survivors, with Photographs and Sketches*, 1912

National Archives
National Maritime Museum
Newcastle Morning Herald and Miner's Advocate (NSW), 15 April 1947
New York Herald, 20 April 1912
New York Sun, 25 April 1912
New York Times, 3 March and 16 April 1912
Nicholas, Anthony, *Key Figures aboard RMS Titanic: Superstars and Scapegoats*, 2022
Northampton Mercury, 24 May 1912
Northern Champion (NSW), 20 April 1935
Nottingham Mercury, 24 May 1912

O'Donnell, Father Edward, *Travelling on Titanic with Father Browne*, 2022
Oldham, Wilton J., *The Ismay Line: The White Star Line and the Ismay Family Story*, 1961

Padfield, Peter, *The Titanic and the Californian*, 1965
Parkes, Dan E., *Titanic Legacy: The Captain, the Daughter and the Spy*, 2025
Patten, Louise, *As Good As Gold*, 2010
Pellow, James, with Kendle, Dorothy, A *Lifetime on the Titanic: the Biography of Edith Haisman, Britain's Oldest Survivor of the Titanic Disaster*, 1995
Pierce, Nicola, *Titanic: True Stories of Her Passengers, Crew and Legacy*, 2018

Rahway Daily Record, 19 April 1912
Rochford Daily Register Gazette, 25 April 1912
Rosenbaum Russell, Edith, *The Wreck of the Titanic: Cassell's Magazine*, 1913
Rostron, Sir Arthur Henry, *Home from the Sea*, 1931
Royal Museums, Greenwich
Russell, Gareth, *The Ship of Dreams: The Sinking of the Titanic and the End of the Edwardian Era*, 2019
Ryers, Phylis, *Rich Men Poor Men: Ryersons on the Titanic*, 2012

Sanford, Helen Behr, *Starboard at Midnight*, 2012
Smithsonian Institution
Society of Naval Architects and Marine Engineers, *Titanic: The Anatomy of a Disaster: A Report from the Marine Forensic Panel*, 1997
Southampton Pictorial (various)
Southern Daily Echo, 17 April 2020
Sphere, 10 June 1911, 20 and 27 April 1912, 15 Jun 1912, 28 December 1912, 19 April 1913 and 23 June 1956
Sports Illustrated, 2 April 2012
Springfield Union, 20 April 1912
Stringer, Craig, *Titanic People*, 2012
Sun, 23 April 1912
Surrey Advertiser and County Times, 20 April 1912

Ticehurst, Brian, *The Titanic's Rescuers: Captain, Sir Arthur Rostron and the Crew of the* Carpathia, 1996
Titanic Commutator: The Journal of Titanic Historical Society
Titanic Historical Society
Titanic International Society
Toronto World, 17 April 1912
Turner, Timothy Paul Duncan, *Legacy of the White Star Line*, 2020

United States Enquiry, *Investigation into the Loss of the SS Titanic*, 1912

Villiers, Alan, *Of Ships and Men: A Personal Anthology* 1962

Wade, Wyn Craig, *The Titanic: End of a Dream*, 1979

Wade, Wyn Craig, *The Titanic: Disaster of a Century*, 2012

Washington Post, 20 April 1912

Welshman, Dr John, *Titanic: The Last Night of a Small Town*, 2012

West Briton and Cornwall Advertiser, 18 April 1912

West MBE, Lt-Commander Frank, *Lifeboat Number Seven*, 1960

Western Star and Roma Advertiser (Queensland), 24 April 1912

Whiteley, Thomas, *Titanic Lecture*

Wilson, Andrew, *Shadow of the Titanic: The Extraordinary Stories of Those Who Survived*, 2012

Winocour, Jack, *The Story of the Titanic, as told by its Survivors*, 1960

Woods, Captain E.A., *White Star Sailing Packets: Historic Society of Lancashire and Cheshire*, 1944

INDEX